# FOUNDATIONS FOR SUCCESS
## Strengthening Your Agency Attorney Office



MIMI LAVER

EDITED BY CLAIRE SANDT
AND SALLY SMALL INADA

AMERICAN BAR ASSOCIATION
CENTER ON CHILDREN AND THE LAW
A PROGRAM OF THE YOUNG LAWYERS DIVISION

AMERICAN BAR ASSOCIATION

CENTER ON CHILDEN AND THE LAW

*Foundations For Success: Strengthening Your Agency Attorney Office*


Library of Congress Cataloging-in-Publication Data

**Laver, Mimi, 1965-**

Foundations for success: strengthening your agency attorney office / Mimi Laver; edited by Claire Sandt; contributors, Janet Chiancone…[et al.].

p. cm.

Includes bibliographical references.

ISBN 1-57073-731-2

1. Children — Legal status, laws, etc. — United States. 2. Child welfare — United States. I. Sandt, Claire. II. Chiancone. Janet. III. title.

KF3735.Z9L38 1999

344.73'0327—dc21 99-38558

CIP



Printed in the United States of America.

Research performed on Westlaw compliments of West Group.

# TABLE OF CONTENTS

*Introduction* . . . . . . . . . . . . . . . . . . . . . . . . . . . . . . i

***Chapter 1: Time To Raise Your Standards:***
A Guide to Developing Agency
Attorney Practice Standards . . . . . . . . . . . . . . . . . . 9

***Chapter 2: So You're Hiring?:***
A Guide to Choosing the Best Candidate. . . . . . . . 29

***Chapter 3: A Guide to Retaining***
***Agency Attorneys*** . . . . . . . . . . . . . . . . . . . . . . . . 47

***Chapter 4: Getting the Most***
***From Performance Evaluations*** . . . . . . . . . . . . 57

***Chapter 5: Teams Within the Team***
San Diego County Counsel
Juvenile Dependency Division. . . . . . . . . . . . . . . . 75

***Chapter 6: Representing the***
***Child Welfare Agency:***
Establishing Caseload Standards . . . . . . . . . . . . . 81

***Chapter 7: Making Life Easier:***
Using All of Your Resources Well. . . . . . . . . . . . . . 91

***Chapter 8:***
***Agency Attorneys and Caseworkers:***
Working Well Together. . . . . . . . . . . . . . . . . . . . . 111

***Chapter 9: Team Spirit***
Santa Clara County Counsel
Office Child Dependency Unit . . . . . . . . . . . . . . . . 131

***Chapter 10: Implementing ASFA:***
A Challenge for Agency Attorneys . . . . . . . . . . . . 137

***Appendix A: In the Workplace:***
The Cost of Caring: Burnout . . . . . . . . . . . . . . . . 159

***Appendix B: Websites to Visit*** . . . . . . . . . . . . . 169

***Appendix C: Helpful Forms***

Child Dependency Unit Office of the County Counsel, Santa Clara County Job Description . . . . . . . . . . 173

Brown Bag Lunch Seminars at the Department of Family & Children's Services . . . . 176

Offsite Program:
Santa Clara County Social Services Agency
Department of Family & Children's Services
Manager, Supervisor and County Counsel . . . . . . 178

Forensic Human Services
A Certificate Program for Human Service Professionals: Program Brochure . . . . . . . . . . . . . 180

San Diego County Counsel
Paternity Tracking Sheet . . . . . . . . . . . . . . . . . . . 194

Office of County Counsel
Juvenile Dependency Division
Performance Evaluations for Attorneys . . . . . . . . 196

Performance Standards: Deputy County Counsel and Senior Deputy County Juvenile Dependency Division Counsel . . . . . . . .204

ICWA Heritage Tree Chart . . . . . . . . . . . . . . . . . .219

# INTRODUCTION

This book acknowledges what you do in representing the agency is hard work. It provides you with ideas on how to set reasonable goals and improve your practice to benefit the agency, children and families.

In 1997, the Adoption and Safe Families Act (ASFA) became law. ASFA challenges all of us to focus on safety and timely permanence for children in our systems. As the legal representative for the agency, you play a key role in ensuring that these themes become a reality in your jurisdiction.

What follows is a series of articles previously published in *Child Law Practice (CLP),* the American Bar Association Center on Children and the Law's monthly reporter. The articles vary in tone. I have chosen to keep the tone of the original articles.

There are a number of models of agency representation. In some areas local prosecutors do the agency's legal work; in other places the agency hires its own lawyers; sometimes private lawyers are on contract and in some places the county or states' attorneys handle the agency's legal matters. Sometimes different offices handle different parts of a case. For simplicity, I use the term "agency attorney" to mean any attorney doing legal work for the child welfare agency.

*In researching this book, I found that the agency attorney offices that seem to be functioning well all had a strong sense of teamwork.*

The attorneys and non-attorney staff seem to work as one unit, supporting each other through good and bad periods. They were willing to stand in for each other in court when necessary and they were willing to listen when their colleagues were feeling blue about cases or life experiences.

Similarly, creating this book was a group effort. The team was made up of ABA staff as well as agency attorneys throughout the country who were constantly willing to share their time and thoughts.

I would like to particularly acknowledge several people. The first is Claire Sandt, the extraordinary editor of the CLP. Claire's patience, vision and ability to edit words without losing meaning were much needed and appreciated. Mark Hardin, the Director of Child Welfare at the Center, saw the need for a book focused on agency representation and ensured its existence. Mark was always willing to discuss and brainstorm ideas to flesh out my thoughts. Sally Small Inada also helped greatly in editing the articles. Even more importantly, she kept me calm in the final aspects of designing the book. Sally's knowledge of production and "nitty gritty" details was amazing.

I also want to thank the rest of the CLP team for helpful and necessary research, editing and sometimes lengthy discussions about wording and concepts. Thanks to Sharon Elstein, Katie Warwick Scrivner, Janet Chiancone and Yolande Samerson. Thanks to Elyse Csillag for all the proofing and computer expertise. Noy Davis designed the beautiful cover for which I am grateful. Thanks also to Big Dog Studios for the excellent graphic designing.

I know, from personal experience, how busy agency attorneys and staff are. For this reason I am particularly grateful to Yvonne Billingsley, Melissa

Mitchell and her staff, Mary Widman and her staff, Patricia Wright, James Anderson, Sherri Kaplan and Mike Rumbaugh for their willingness to be interviewed, review articles and provide constructive criticism. I am also very thankful that Diane Bennett and Mike Clark and their staff at the County Counsel office of San Jose, Susan Strom, Gary Seiser, Kathryn Krug and the entire team at the County Counsel office in San Diego and Judge James Milliken were willing to share their time and honesty with me. Thanks also to Judge Len Edwards for his insights and the concept of a California site visit.

This book, and the article series on which it was based, would not have been possible without the U.S. Department of Health and Human Services, Administration for Children and Youth's grant to the National Resource Center on Legal and Court Issues. I wish to extend a special thank you to Emily Cooke, the grant's project officer, for her commitment to improving legal representation in the child welfare system and her strong support of our work.

Representing a child welfare agency can be both a pleasure and a challenge. Resources are scarce, legal mandates are imposing, the subject matter is sad and sometimes personalities clash. The positive impact you can have on children and families, though, can outweigh all of the difficulties. You know improving agency representation is a step-by-step process. Dramatic change will not happen immediately, but it will happen.

CHAPTER 1:

# Time to Raise Your Standards:

A GUIDE TO DEVELOPING AGENCY ATTORNEY PRACTICE STANDARDS

Children's attorneys have practice standards. Judges have practice standards. Shouldn't *you?*

This chapter looks at practice standards for agency attorneys – why have them, how to develop them, and what they could look like. The suggestions and tips offered here are a springboard to get you started. Since agency attorney standards do not seem to exist in the field, you will be ahead of the game if you take a crack at them.

## WHY HAVE STANDARDS?

Develop practice standards to:

### Improve the Quality of Representation

One important outcome of developing practice standards is raising the quality of representation. Children, families, and child welfare agencies deserve high quality representation in abuse and neglect cases. In many areas, you may discover the quality of representation is not what it should be.

Standards can help define quality representation and give attorneys goals to strive towards.

### Ensure Uniformity of Practice

Standards should lead to uniform practices. When there is consistency in attorneys' representation, the agency benefits. Caseworkers will know and appreciate that no matter which attorney they call with a question or handles their case in court, they will receive high-quality representation. This can improve their confidence and desire to work as a team with attorneys.

### Promote Professionalism

As they achieve the goal of the high level representation described in the standards, agency attorneys' feelings about the job, client, and court system may become more positive. With improved representation comes respect by others in the system. As a result, the level of professionalism in the attorneys' office will rise.

### Identify and Increase Resources

Analyzing current practices and deciding what improvements should be in place can help you determine what resources, both people and technical, are needed to deliver better legal services. Agency attorney caseloads are notoriously high. Some agency attorneys lack computers, voice mail, adequate support staff (i.e. legal and administrative assistants) and other resources to improve work efficiency. Developing standards can help you assess where resources are lacking. This can help you make a strong case for an increase in staff or more resources.

## HOW TO DEVELOP STANDARDS

### Form a Committee

The committee should be diverse, but be a manageable size. If the standards will apply to agency attorneys throughout the state, involve representatives from courts, agencies and the bar across the state. If the standards will apply to one location, involve local representatives.

Include as many stakeholders as possible, especially those in authority positions, so the end product will be respected and supported. Involve agency attorneys, attorney supervisors, and agency administrators. Consider inviting judges, caseworkers, parent and children's attorneys, court administrators, a foster care review board member, and someone from the Human Services Board. For a neutral voice, invite a state Court Improvement Program representative or a local law professor.

Consider if a committee already exists that might be willing to take on the task of developing standards (e.g. a court improvement committee). This might save time in forming a new committee.

Another way to design standards is by holding a conference. The Georgia Court Improvement Program successfully used this approach to develop guidelines for its courts and judges. It hopes to do the same for its special assistant attorneys general (SAAGs). It is now organizing a conference that will bring together 10 SAAGs to develop standards for the SAAGs throughout Georgia.[1]

### Conduct an Assessment

Find out the level of representation agency attorneys now provide. Ask attorneys and other stakeholders what is happening in practice, both good and bad. Together, arrive at a common understanding of what "competent"[2] representation means. You may learn the attorneys already do many of the things that will be set forth in the standards. It helps to know that before writing the standards.

### Study Caseloads

Chief among barriers are caseloads. Most agency attorneys have such high caseloads that they are unable to perform at the highest possible level. If this

*Most agency attorneys have such high caseloads that they are unable to perform at the highest possible level. If this is true in your jurisdiction, think about remedies.*

is true in your jurisdiction, think about remedies. Attorneys who strive to perform at the level the standards dictate will be unable to do so if they have too many cases. Find out about caseloads and other barriers to implementing standards.

### Write the Standards

Once the committee has a good idea what elements standards should include, the writing can begin. Decide if you want comprehensive standards, or if you want to start small, for example by focusing just on court practice. Consider dividing the standards into sections with subcommittees writing individual sections and the entire committee approving the end product.

After making these and similar decisions, begin writing. Remember to write in easy-to-understand language so there are no interpretation disputes down the road. Language must be concise and meaningful to your court community. The document should be accessible so the agency attorneys and the agency can and will use it.

### Sell Your Standards

Getting "buy in" from practitioners can be difficult since many are overworked and may resist change. It helps to get the support of professionals in positions of authority, such as child welfare agency administrators, district attorneys, judges, and others. Help them see the value of the standards and how they can be used to guide practice. If practitioners see that others are embracing the standards, they may be more inclined to change their behavior. Selling standards may take time, but it can happen.

## WHAT THE STANDARDS COULD LOOK LIKE

Standards should inspire but be realistic. They should guide the attorneys toward better practice. To the extent possible, they should also be measurable.

The following sample standards are based on the *American Bar Association Standards of Practice for Lawyers Who Represent Children in Abuse and Neglect Cases.*[3] They have been adapted for agency attorneys. Again, they are only meant to get you started developing your own. You may choose a different format and many of your guidelines may differ from those that follow.

### A. Definitions

***A-1 Agency*** — The state or county child welfare agency, sometimes known as the Department of Human Services (DHS), or the Department of Social Services (DSS). The agency is charged with the protection and care of children suspected or found to be abused or neglected and is generally the moving party in abuse or neglect proceedings.

***Commentary*** — It is important to define this term in a jurisdiction-specific manner.

***A-2 Agency Attorney*** — The term "agency attorney" means an agency attorney or agency

*Standards should inspire but be realistic. They should guide the attorneys toward better practice.*

representative including any government attorney, district attorney, attorney general, state attorney, city solicitor or attorney, corporation counsel, or privately retained special prosecutor who represents the petitioner or moving party in an abuse or neglect proceeding.

*Commentary* — Defining this term for your jurisdiction is critical. Everyone should be clear on which attorneys are covered by the practice standards and who the client is.

**B. General Authority and Duties**

***B-1 Basic Obligations*** — The agency attorney should:

- ❑ Fully understand all relevant federal and state laws, regulations and policies affecting child welfare and other related areas;
- ❑ Prepare or help prepare the initial petition and all subsequent pleadings;
- ❑ File all pleadings and motions in a timely fashion;
- ❑ Thoroughly prepare for all hearings;
- ❑ Prepare or help prepare findings of fact and conclusions of law;
- ❑ Participate in all depositions, negotiations, discovery, pretrial conferences, mediation sessions and hearings;
- ❑ Attempt to reduce case delays and ensure the court recognizes the importance of timely permanence for children;
- ❑ Counsel the client/agency concerning all matters related to individual cases as well as develop policy that conforms to federal and state laws;
- ❑ Develop a case theory and strategy to follow at hearings and negotiations;

- ❑ Oversee the agency's efforts to ensure speedy case resolution, such as searches for parents and kin, and applying for necessary documentation;
- ❑ Cooperate and communicate with other professionals and parties in a case.

***Commentary*** — This list is not comprehensive but gives you an idea of some of the aspects of the agency attorney's role. The agency attorney has many tasks to perform. An initial section of the standards should define these roles.

***B-2 Conflict Situations*** — When an agency attorney and an agency caseworker disagree about the best way to handle a case, each should consult his or her supervisor for assistance. If necessary, supervisors should consult and proceed further up the chain of command to reach an agreeable resolution.

***Commentary*** — A conflict resolution system should be in place before conflict occurs. The goal is for the attorneys and caseworkers to work as a team to reach the best outcomes for children and families. Depending on your jurisdiction's model of representation, your conflict resolution system may differ from the one proposed above.

### C. Actions to be Taken

***C-1 Meet with the Agency Caseworker/ Client*** — The agency attorney should be involved in a case from the start. Regular contact with agency representatives is necessary to file complete pleadings, thoroughly prepare for trial and move the case through the judicial system. Open lines of communication between attorneys and caseworkers helps ensure caseworkers get answers to questions and attorneys get information and documents they need.[4]

***Commentary*** — Whether the attorneys in your jurisdiction represent the agency or the state, the caseworkers often have the information needed to put together a strong case. Therefore, the attorneys and caseworkers must meet/communicate regularly. Have a communication system in place. This could involve having office hours when the caseworkers can visit and ask questions, or designating an attorney to take caseworkers' telephone calls.

***C-2 Develop a Case Timeline or Tickler System*** — When a case begins, the agency attorney should develop a legal case plan emphasizing what actions should be taken and when. The attorney should consider federal and state timelines. For example, under the *Adoption and Safe Families Act*, the attorney will need to file a termination of parental rights petition when the child has been in care for 15 of 22 months, unless certain exceptions apply. The attorney should know when the 15 month point is and whether any exceptions apply.

***Commentary*** — Agency attorneys handle many cases at a time and must be organized to juggle them all. A good calendaring system, implemented at the beginning and throughout each case, can help the attorneys better manage their cases.

***C-3 Obtain the Information You Need*** — Generally, attorneys will get necessary documentation from the caseworker's file. This file should include full mental health and substance abuse treatment records and histories, abuse and neglect reports with supporting materials about the investigation, birth certificates for the children, death certificates, affidavits of efforts to locate parents, and paternity test results.

If the information needed to prepare a pleading or for a trial is not in the record, the attorney should either ask the caseworker to order it or request it him or herself. The attorney may need to request a court order to obtain this material.

***Commentary*** — Strong exhibits and documentary evidence can make or break a case. It is the attorney's obligation to ensure all relevant information is brought to the court's attention. At times, that means personally getting the documents. It may also mean requesting an order from the judge so the agency may obtain what might otherwise be confidential documents.

***C-4 File Pleadings*** — As the legal representative for the moving party, the agency attorney needs to file petitions (including termination of parental rights petitions), various motions, discovery requests, and responses and answers to pleadings filed by other parties. These pleadings must be thorough, accurate and timely.

***C-5 Negotiate Settlements*** — The agency attorney should participate in settlement negotiations to seek speedy resolution of the case, keeping in mind the effect of continuances and delays on the child. However, the child's safety must not be negotiated away. The attorney should use mediation resources when available.

***Commentary*** — Negotiation and mediation often result in a detailed agreement among parties of actions that must be taken by all participants. Generally, all parties feel like they had a say in these arrangements and are, therefore, more willing to adhere to a plan. Negotiated settlements generally happen quicker than full hearings and therefore move a case along in a reasonable time period. Agency attorneys should be trained in negotiation skills and be comfortable resolving cases outside a courtroom setting.

It is important, though, for the attorney to keep the agency's position in mind while negotiating. There are things that cannot be compromised (e.g., the child's safety or the key underlying facts of the case) and all parties should be aware of them. The attorney must be willing to try the case and not compromise on every point to avoid the hearing.

***C-6 Subpoena and Prepare Witnesses*** — The agency attorney should develop a witness list well before a hearing. Witnesses, especially those from outside the agency, may need ample warning about the date and time of the trial so they can be present. The attorney should, when possible, call the witness and let him or her know a subpoena is on its way. Then, the attorney should make arrangements to have the subpoena served.

Attorneys should reserve time to prepare all witnesses in person before the hearing. Some witnesses may require written questions. These should be provided.

***Commentary*** — Preparation is the key to successfully resolving a case, either in negotiation or trial. The attorney should plan as early as possible for the case and make arrangements accordingly. Doctors, nurses, teachers, therapists and other potential witnesses have busy schedules and need advanced warning about the date and time of the hearing. Witnesses are often nervous about testifying in court. Attorneys should therefore prepare witnesses thoroughly so they feel comfortable with the process and the questions they will likely be asked.

### D. Hearings

***D-1 Court Appearances*** — The agency attorney should attend and be prepared for all hearings and participate in all phone or other court conferences. At a minimum, adequate preparation requires communicating with the agency before the hearing, preparing witnesses before the hearing, preparing exhibits, and conducting legal research.

***Commentary*** — If the agency is to be well represented, the agency attorney must be prepared and present in court. Even in jurisdictions where the agency attorney represents the state, the attorney must be active in the court process to protect children and ensure their safety. There are jurisdictions in which a nonattorney representative from the agency appears in court on uncontested matters. If this is how your system works, it should be noted in the standards and an attorney should be available if the case becomes complicated.

***D-2 Client and Witness Explanation*** — The agency attorney should clearly explain to the caseworker and the witnesses what is expected to happen before, during and after each hearing.

***D-3 Motions and Objections*** — The agency attorney should make appropriate motions and evidentiary objections to advance the agency's position during the hearing. If necessary, the agency attorney should file briefs supporting the agency's position on evidentiary issues. The agency attorney should preserve legal issues for appeal.

***D-4 Presentation of Evidence*** — The agency attorney must present and cross-examine witnesses and prepare and present exhibits.

***Commentary*** — Because the agency is the moving party in most hearings, the burden is on the agency attorney to present a solid case with well-prepared witnesses and documentary evidence. Additionally, it is important that the agency attorney is comfortable cross-examining witnesses when the other parties present their cases.

***D-5 Child Witnesses*** — The agency attorney should consult with the agency caseworker and the child's attorney to decide whether the child should be present and testify at a hearing. The decision should be based on the child's best interests and emotional well being. Attorneys must consider the child's wishes, any possible effects on the child of the testimony, and the child's ability to handle cross-examination. The agency attorney and child's attorney should decide who will present the child's testimony.

If the child is called to testify during the agency's case-in-chief, opposing parties and the judge may agree to allow the child's attorney to conduct the direct examination to make the child more comfortable. The judge may also agree to hear the child in chambers so the child does not have to testify in front of the parents. In a civil action, there is no absolute right to confrontation. If the parents' attorneys are present to hear the child's testimony, the parents' rights will be protected.

Questions posed to the child must be clear and developmentally appropriate.[5]

***Commentary*** — Generally, the child should be present at the hearings because the proceeding concerns the child's life and the child's input must be considered. However, if the child will be traumatized by the experience, he or she should not be present in court.

***D-6 Jury Selection*** — In jurisdictions in which a jury trial is possible, the agency attorney must participate in jury selection and help draft jury instructions.

***D-7 Conclusion of Hearing*** — The agency attorney should make a closing argument and provide proposed findings of fact and conclusions of law. The agency attorney should ensure a written order is entered and provided to the agency.

### E. Post-Hearing

***E-1 Review Order with Agency*** — After the hearing, the agency attorney and caseworker should review the written order to ensure it reflects the court's verbal order and the caseworker understands what is required. If the order is controversial, or the caseworker is unhappy with it, the agency attorney should review it with the caseworker's supervisor and potentially the agency's administration and the attorney's supervisor.

***E-2 Implementation*** — The agency attorney should monitor the agency's efforts to implement the order and answer any questions the caseworker may have about the agency's obligations under the order.

***Commentary*** — E-1 and E-2 illustrate the importance of the agency attorney's role outside the courtroom. The attorney should help the agency understand and follow through with the court's orders to protect the agency, but more importantly to ensure the agency provides the best possible services for children and families.

### F. Appeals

***F-1 Decision to Appeal*** — The agency attorney should consider and discuss with the agency caseworker and supervisor the possibility of appeal when a court's ruling is against the agency's position or interests. If the agency decides to appeal, and the appeal has merit, the agency attorney must file the necessary post-hearing motions and the notice to appeal paperwork in a timely fashion.

In jurisdictions in which an attorney other than the agency attorney handles the appeal, the agency attorney should identify issues that are appropriate for appeal and work with the new attorney on the appeal. As the attorney who handled the trial, the agency attorney may have insight beyond what the new attorney could get by reading the trial transcript.

***Commentary*** — When discussing the possibility of an appeal, the attorney should explain both the positive and negative effects of an appeal. For instance, an appeal might unnecessarily delay a case or might make "bad law" for future cases in which the agency participates. Conversely, if a judge made a poor decision that negatively impacts the child's future and his or her chance at permanency, an appeal should be taken.

***F-2 While the Appeal is Pending*** — The agency attorney must carefully review his or her obligations in the state's Rules of Appellate Procedure. The attorney must file all paperwork, including requests for transcript and case file, in a timely fashion. If the state court allows, the attorney should request an expedited appeal. In this request, outline why the case should be expedited (e.g., any special characteristics about the child). The appellate brief must be concise, comprehensive, and timely filed. If arguments are scheduled, the attorney must prepare thoroughly.

***Commentary*** — Appellate skills differ from the skills most agency attorneys use day to day. The agency attorney may wish to seek guidance from an experienced appellate advocate when drafting the brief and preparing for argument. An appeal can have a great deal of impact on the trial judge who heard the case and in trial courts throughout the state. The request for an expedited appeal should always be considered. Appeals hold up the process a great deal and whatever can be done to allow the child's case to be moved forward should be done. The attorney should take great care during the appellate process.

***F-3 Conclusion of Appeal*** — The agency attorney must communicate the result and its effects to the agency. If as a result of the appeal the agency needs to take action in the case, it should be instructed to do so. If as a result of the appeal the attorney needs to file any motions with the trial court, the attorney must do so.

## G. Managing the Office

***G-1 Caseloads*** — Determine reasonable caseload levels for agency attorneys. Be sure to have a consistent definition of what a "case" is: a family or a child. When assessing the appropriate number, remember to account for all of the agency attorney's obligations, the difficulty of cases, and the need for adequate time to thoroughly prepare cases. Once caseload levels are set, stick with them and ensure attorneys do not exceed them. For more information see chapter six.

***Commentary*** — High caseload is considered one of the major barriers to quality representation and a source of high attorney turnover. It is essential to decide what a reasonable and doable caseload is in your jurisdiction. How attorneys define cases and attorney obligations vary from place-to-place, but no matter where you are, having a manageable caseload is absolutely necessary. One study found that a caseload of 40-50 active cases is reasonable, and a caseload of over 60 cases is unmanageable.[6] These numbers may provide you with guidance as you think about caseloads.

***G-2 Technical and Staff Support*** — The agency attorney must have adequate and operational equipment to do the high level job these standards describe. Quality staff support is also essential. The office should have qualified legal assistants and administrative assistants to help the agency attorney. For more information see chapter seven.

***Commentary*** — The agency attorney cannot do a good job when he or she spends a lot of time trying to get the copy machine to work. The attorney must at least have access to a good quality computer, voice mail, fax machine and copier to get the work done efficiently and with as little stress as possible. Also, by employing qualified staff, the attorney will be freed to do the essentials of representation. For instance, a legal assistant can do research, help draft petitions, schedule and help prepare witnesses and more.

***G-3 Brief and Forms Banks*** — Develop standard briefs, memorandum of law and forms that attorneys can use, so they do not "reinvent the wheel" for each new project. These include: sample discovery request forms, motions, notice of appeal, and petitions. Similarly, memorandum of law and appellate briefs follow certain patterns the attorney could copy and only require filling in specific facts about a case. These forms and briefs should be available in computer format and hard copy. For more information see chapter seven.

***G-4 Training and Education*** — Each agency attorney should participate in training and education programs. Training should include general legal topics, such as regular updates on evidence and trial skills, and child welfare-specific topics, such as:

- ❑ Termination of parental rights law
- ❑ Legal permanency options

- ❑ Adoption subsidies
- ❑ Developmental psychology
- ❑ Talking with children in language they understand
- ❑ Failure to thrive– how to diagnose and what it means
- ❑ Negotiation strategies and techniques
- ❑ Mental illness
- ❑ Substance abuse
- ❑ How domestic violence impacts children

When appropriate, joint training for attorneys and social work staff should be held. Joint training can help strengthen relationships between social workers and attorneys and prevent future conflicts. For more information see chapters three and eight.

***Commentary*** — Agency attorneys should be encouraged to learn as much as possible and participate in conferences and trainings to expand their understanding of developments in the child welfare field. While agency attorneys are often overworked and do not have the extra time to attend conferences, the knowledge they gain will be invaluable. The philosophy of the office should stress the need for ongoing learning and professional growth.

***G-5 Hiring Process*** — Efforts should be made to hire highly qualified attorneys. When possible, hiring decisions should be made by committee. The hiring committee should decide what qualities agency attorneys should possess. Hiring criteria may include: educational and professional achievements; experience and commitment to the child welfare field; interpersonal skills; diversity and the needs of the office; writing and verbal skills; and ability to handle pressure. To choose the best possible candidates, advertise positions widely, conduct thorough interviews and post-interview discussions, and check references. For more information see chapter two.

***Commentary*** — Hiring top attorneys is essential to raising the level of representation and the level of services the agency receives. The agency attorney job is a difficult one — there are many tasks to complete in a short period of time — and the agency attorney often moves the rest of the system. With strong, committed attorneys, the system can drastically improve.

***G-6 Evaluation Process*** — Develop an evaluation process. This system should focus on consistency, constructive criticism and improvement. Some factors to evaluate include: moving cases to permanency at a good pace; preparation and trial skills; ability to work with agency and other professionals; and ability to work as a team player. For more information see chapter four.

***Commentary*** — A solid attorney evaluation process will enable the attorneys to know what they should be working on, what management believes are priorities, what they are doing well and where they need improvement. If a positive process is created, the attorneys will feel supported in their positions and empowered to make improvements as time goes on.

***G-7 Salary*** — The agency attorney's salary should be competitive with other government attorneys in the jurisdiction.

***Commentary*** — While resources are scarce, agency attorneys deserve to be paid a competitive wage. To work in the child welfare field, they are surely dedicated, however, they will not be able to stay in their position, nor be motivated to work harder, without a reasonable salary. High attorney turnover can be decreased when attorneys are paid well.

## CONCLUSION

Agency attorney practice standards can improve agency representation, lead to uniform practices, and increase professionalism. They may also help secure needed resources. This chapter is a starting point and is meant only as a guide. Standards should be tailored to meet specific needs within your jurisdiction. Including attorneys and other stakeholders in the process can help ensure standards are meaningful and will be used. The result could go a long way to improve the child welfare system.

* Special thanks to Patricia Wright, Assistant District Legal Counsel, Pensacola, FL, Mary Widmann, Supervising Attorney and staff attorney, New Orleans, LA, and Yvonne Billingsley, Cleveland, OH for their helpful reviews of earlier drafts.

## ENDNOTES

1. Telephone Interview with Michelle Barclay, Project Director of the Supreme Court of Georgia Child Placement Project, Atlanta, GA, January 7, 1999.

2. Rule 1.1 and 1.3 and commentary. *Model Rules of Professional Conduct*. Chicago: American Bar Association, 1997. ("A lawyer shall provide competent representation to a client. Competent representation requires the legal knowledge, skill, thoroughness and preparation reasonably necessary for representation." 1.1 and "A lawyer shall act with reasonable diligence and promptness in representing a client." 1.3.)

3. *American Bar Association Standards of Practice for Lawyers Who Represent Children in Abuse and Neglect Case*. Approved by the American Bar Association House of Delegates, February 5, 1996.

4. Rule 1.4 and commentary. *Model Rules of Professional Conduct.* ("Communication").

5. *American Bar Association Standards of Practice for Lawyers Who Represent Children in Abuse and Neglect Case*. D-5 – D-9.

CHAPTER 2:

# So You're Hiring?

A GUIDE TO CHOOSING THE BEST CANDIDATE

You're asked to start the hiring process to fill the shoes of an attorney who left your office for another job. Do you take the easy route and hire the first person who comes through the door? Or, do you see the assignment as a chance to hire someone who has what it takes to represent the agency — someone who will work well with your staff, is passionate about protecting children and families, and provides quality legal representation?

Make the right choice and hire the best attorney you can find. This chapter will give you concrete hiring strategies that will make a difference. Read on to learn how.

## THE HIRING PROCESS

### Form a Hiring Committee

When making an important decision, it is valuable to have a group involved. The hiring process can only be aided by group decisionmaking.

Identify a team to serve as the ongoing hiring committee. This group is charged with locating, identifying and hiring the best candidate. Committee members must have time to prepare, interview potential candidates and make hiring decisions. The members must include at least one person with authority to extend the offer, possibly one caseworker or agency administrator and several attorneys in the office. Committee members should include people who will have ongoing contact with the new attorney.

They should have diverse backgrounds, have positive feelings about the job and be good decisionmakers.[1]

## Decide What the Agency is Looking For in a Candidate: Hiring Criteria

The committee must decide what qualities and special skills it hopes to find in a candidate. Start by considering the following skills, and adding any additional qualities you believe are essential for the job:

### *Educational and Professional Achievements*

Educational achievements should be considered, even though grades in law school and college are not the only indicator of a bright and motivated individual. The individual's major or area of study should also be considered. A person who was motivated enough to pursue academic challenges and do well is probably the type of person the committee would want to consider.

Also, an individual who concentrated his or her studies in a related area, such as psychology, education, or sociology, demonstrates a longstanding interest and probable commitment to children and families. Also consider whether the candidate has published any related articles or had strong litigation experience since finishing school.

### *Experience and Commitment to the Field*

Strive to find a candidate who has had some job or volunteer experience involving children or families. Such activities might include education, social work, pediatric medicine, public interest legal jobs, tutoring or running an after-school sports clinic.

The number of years the individual has spent in the child welfare field is also a factor to consider. By including these experiences on the list of desired qualities you are more likely to find someone committed to the field. When representing the agency, many difficult situations arise. The agency attorney must be able to handle these situations, both emotionally and intellectually. Someone who is dedicated to the practice and the children involved is better able to cope with the pressure and provide consistently good representation.

### *Ability to Get Along with People*

The attorney will be in contact with social workers of varied backgrounds and experience levels, attorneys, judges, professionals in education, medicine and the mental health field, as well as often confused and distraught family members. To best represent the agency, the attorney must work with and negotiate with these people in a positive manner.

### *Creative Thinker*

The attorney must also be able to think broadly and have the ability to resolve problems in a nonconfrontational way. If the attorney is able to view a problem or a court case from different perspectives, there is a greater likelihood that the resolution will benefit the agency as well as the other parties.

### *Community Needs and Diversity*

The hiring committee should determine if particular community needs exist that must be addressed. For example, is there a substantial portion of the community that is Spanish speaking? If so, should the attorney also be Spanish speaking? Is the office made up of a culturally diverse staff? When people of varied backgrounds work together and share ideas, the work product is better and therefore the quality of representation is better.[2]

### *Additional Factors*

In addition you should consider these qualities:

- ❑ writing ability
- ❑ verbal ability
- ❑ ability to work within a bureaucracy
- ❑ ability to handle pressure and emotional situations
- ❑ energy and enthusiasm

## Create a Job Description

Once the hiring committee determines what qualities they want in a new attorney they should create a job description. The description must be accurate and completely explain the job responsibilities. A thorough job description and a list of desired qualities will help the committee search for and identify the best individual for the job. (See next page).

## Decide Where to Look for the Candidate

### *Write and place an ad*

Getting a strong and varied pool of applicants involves "getting the word out." Begin writing an ad for the job by reviewing the list of desired qualities and the job description. The ad should clearly explain the job and emphasize that it deals with child abuse and neglect. It should plainly set forth the required

---

*The hiring committee should determine if particular community needs exist that must be addressed. For example, is there a substantial portion of the community that is Spanish speaking?*

---

## Sample Job Description

An entry level attorney position consists of the following duties and responsibilities:

- Representing the agency in court in all steps of the legal process from emergency hearing through termination of parental rights proceedings
- Working with the legal assistants to draft petitions and motions
- Filing termination of parental rights petitions
- Taking appeals when needed: writing the brief and arguing in appellate court
- Answering caseworkers' questions and providing legal advice — supervisors will assist
- Attending trainings both in and out of the office
- Attending meetings with caseworkers concerning individual cases
- Attending task force meetings as requested by supervisor
- Keeping up-to-date on relevant law
- Acting as an emergency duty attorney in rotation with colleagues

and desired qualifications. Include a salary range so applicants are not surprised later in the process. (See example, p. 2–35).

### *Spread the Word*

Once you are satisfied with the ad, distribute it widely. Place the ad in local and national newspapers. When choosing newspapers, think about which ones will reach a range of people in different parts of the community. Consider national publications that list public sector job openings, and web sites or Internet postings. Possible places to post your ad are:

- ❑ your local bar association may have a newsletter
- ❑ your state bar association probably has a *Lawyer's Weekly*
- ❑ *The Guardian* — published quarterly by the National Association of Counsel for Children (NACC)
- ❑ The University of Michigan/ NACC Child Law and Advocacy National Job Web Site: www.law.umich.edu; call 734/763-5598 to post positions.
- ❑ *Front Line Views* — published quarterly by the National Family Preservation Network

Another part of advertising the job is actually spreading the word verbally. Talk with members of the local child welfare community, including judges, about the opening. While the goal is not to give jobs to unqualified friends, these community members may know high quality candidates. Similarly, be sure to contact former interns or volunteer attorneys who did good work in the office.[3] They may need jobs or know people who are also interested in work in the field.

## Sample Ad: Wanted!

Attorney to represent local child welfare agency in child abuse and neglect cases. Applicant must have two years experience, preferably in a related position. Applicant must also have strong educational background and writing skills. Candidate must be committed to the field and be able to work with a varied group of people. Candidate must be a creative thinker, must be able to think well on his or her feet and must work well under pressure. A candidate who speaks Spanish would be preferred. A new attorney in our office should already be or be willing to familiarize self with child welfare statutes, regulations and policy. This individual should expect to spend a good deal of time in court and with child welfare social workers. Please send resume and writing sample. Salary range: $34,000-40,000*; excellent benefits.

*Salaries will vary depending on location.

### *Contact Law Schools*

Finally, law schools are a good way to identify quality applicants. Schools generally have placement offices that alumni use during job searches. Some law schools throughout the country have clinical programs in child advocacy or child welfare issues. Participants of these programs have already demonstrated an interest in the field and may be just the type of people the committee wants to hire.

## Finding the Right Candidate

### *Pre-Interview*

Once resumes start coming into the office, it is time to decide which candidates to interview. Begin by carefully reviewing the cover letter and resume. Most applicants will not possess all the qualities on the initial list, but the letter and resume can provide a good sense of the candidate's past experience and commitment. The resume will suggest certain characteristics about the applicant, such as:

- ❑ progression of job responsibilities
- ❑ factors that influenced job selection
- ❑ number of jobs held
- ❑ writing ability
- ❑ whether or not the person worked while attending school
- ❑ willingness to travel
- ❑ ability and experience supervising others
- ❑ any time gaps between jobs
- ❑ numerous job changes
- ❑ inconsistency or lack of work experience[4]

From the resume, choose candidates who seem to possess the desired skills and qualities. Also, use the resume to create questions for the interview.

### *Choose an Interview Format*

Next, decide how to structure the interviews — panel interviews or one-on-one. If a panel interview is chosen, decide who should sit on the panel. Consider asking a caseworker or agency administrator to be a panel member. While this may be a shift in "the way things have always been done," the clients may feel pleased to be invited. In other legal situations, the clients may meet several attorneys before hiring one. There is no reason the agency should not be treated as any other client in this situation. Also, having someone from the agency on the panel sends a clear message to the applicant that the attorneys value the agency client's input.

If a one-on-one interview is chosen, consider whether to have the candidate meet several staff members one after the other, or if one interview will be enough as a first interview. Decide how second interviews will be handled and who will conduct them.

### *Develop Interview Questions*

The next step is to develop a list of questions to ask all the candidates. There are different types of questions to consider:

*Open-ended questions* are designed to elicit complete responses, opinions and feelings, rather than short, nondetailed responses. These questions generally start with words like "how," "describe," "tell me," "compare." Some examples of these questions are: (1) Tell me about any presentations you have had to make in front of other people; (2) Describe a difficult experience from your current position; (3) What has been your experience working with demanding personalities; (4) What are you hoping to learn and achieve through this position; (5) What

*When satisfied with the information obtained from the candidate, one interviewer should speak honestly about the position. The candidate should hear both the positives and negatives about the job: types of cases, a realistic account of the caseload the new attorney would handle, job responsibilities, and information about the staff.*

qualities do you possess that you believe will be helpful in this position.

Interviewers should avoid questions that might make the applicant defensive, such as questions that begin with "why?" The majority of questions asked during an interview should be open-ended.[5]

*Situational questions* reveal how the candidate might resolve issues or problems that typically arise on the job. The questions should be brief hypothetical questions concerning cases or interpersonal situations, such as conflicts with social workers. The questions should elicit specific ways the candidate would attempt to resolve the dilemma and demonstrate problem-solving skills.[6]

For example: You are preparing a sexual abuse case for the fact finding hearing. You believe the case is legally difficult to prove and think the child will need to testify. The social worker does not think the child should be brought to court. How would you handle this situation?

Be sure to avoid potentially discriminatory questions (see next page). Once committee members

# Do's and Don'ts of Interviewing

## FIVE DO'S

1. Press for Specifics
2. Allow Silence
3. Maintain Control
4. Look for Contrary Evidence
5. Avoid Evaluative Feedback — verbal or non-verbal

## TEN DON'TS

1. Being unprepared
2. Excessive Socializing
3. Interruption
4. Excessive Note-Taking
5. Doing Other Work During the Interview
6. Answering Your Own Questions
7. Rapid-Fire Questions
8. Talking Too Much
9. Violating a Regulation of Equal Employment Opportunity (EEO)
10. Leading Questions

Source: ABA CEELI Porgram Interviewing Skills Training: Selecting the Right Candidate, Section II, 1-2.

are comfortable with all of the questions, decide who will ask them.

### *Schedule the Interviews*

All interviewers should review their schedules and identify at least one hour blocks of time during which their full attention can be devoted to the interview. Then candidates should be contacted to schedule the interviews.

### *The Interview*

The interview will help you gain information about the candidate, observe how the candidate interacts with people, and learn how the candidate would function in the job. When the candidate first enters the interview room, introduce everyone and spend a few minutes in "small talk." By trying to ease the candidate and build rapport, there is a greater chance of assessing the individual's natural behaviors. (See box p. 2–39 for interviewing do's and don'ts.)

After a few minutes, begin the substantive section of the interview. Start by asking open-ended questions designed to gather important facts about the applicant. Use this time to fill in any gaps in the person's resume. Encourage the candidate to give specific information rather than generalities and to expand fully on the answers. When the interviewer moves on to ask the situational questions, the candidate should also have the opportunity to provide full answers.

When satisfied with the information obtained from the candidate, one interviewer should speak honestly about the position. The candidate should hear both the positives and negatives about the job: types of cases, a realistic account of the caseload the new attorney would handle, job responsibilities, and information about the staff. Also, consider talking briefly about salary and benefits. A candidate deserves to know what the job will entail. Full disclosure helps prevent hiring an attorney only to find out he or she is not able to handle the job. If all parties are honest from the beginning, hopefully the best candidate will be chosen.

Next, give the candidate a chance to ask questions. Answer the candidate's questions as honestly as possible. The types of questions asked will reveal a great deal about the candidate, so be careful not to "tune out" or feel the interview is over until the candidate actually leaves.

When all questions are answered, explain what happens next in the process. For example, state when the candidate can expect to hear from the office and whether there will be additional interviews. End the interview with more small talk and escort the candidate to the exit.

### *Post-interview*

Make notes and evaluate the candidate as soon as the interview is over. This will help you and the other interviewers remember important reactions to the candidate, prevent confusing the candidates, and protect against possible discrimination concerns later on.[7] The evaluations should be guided by the list of desired qualities developed by the committee before the interviews.

After all candidates have been interviewed, the committee should meet and discuss the candidates. Using the criteria established when writing the job description as a guide, try to evaluate the candidates to determine which one best fits the "ideal candidate" model.

The following factors are less objective, but may also influence the decision to hire a new attorney:

*1.* ***The Cringe Factor*** — What were the candidate's responses — both verbal and nonverbal — to the interview discussion about abuse and neglect cases the office handles? Did the candidate appear interested, committed and emotionally able to handle it or too nervous? Was the candidate able to articulate an ability to handle the subject matter?

*2.* ***The Team-player Factor*** — How did the interviewers feel the candidate would work with others in the office? While friendships in the office are not the issue, colleagues need to support each other, especially in an office that handles such serious and upsetting cases. Did the candidate seem willing to help others in the office?

*3.* ***The Resilience Factor*** — How did the candidate seem to handle pressure?

Would the candidate be able to leave the sad cases in the office or would he or she be plagued by them? After a hard day in court, would the candidate be able to return to the office the next day with a fresh outlook?

While these subjective factors should not be the primary considerations in choosing the new attorney, the committee should feel comfortable trusting their judgment and using these criteria when deciding between qualified candidates.

### Check References and Make an Offer

After identifying a first choice candidate, a committee member should contact the candidate's references. When talking with the reference, first ask questions to verify information such as job title and amount of time at the job.

Next ask questions that are fact specific concerning the candidate's responsibilities, strengths and work quality. Such questions could include:

- ❑ How would you describe the candidate's court performance?
- ❑ Does the candidate supervise other attorneys?
- ❑ Tell me about the candidate's supervisory skills?
- ❑ What were the candidate's achievements while working with you?
- ❑ What could the candidate do for ongoing professional growth and development?

Listen carefully not only to what the reference says but how it is said. Consider whether the person enthusiastically provides positive information or whether there are hesitations.[8]

If after speaking with the references you still want to hire the candidate, call him or her and make an offer. During the conversation, there are certain things the candidate needs to know such as:

- ❑ salary and benefits
- ❑ office expectations (e.g., work hours)
- ❑ actual responsibilities
- ❑ expected duties with respect to the agency/client
- ❑ training expectations and requirements
- ❑ emergency duty responsibilities
- ❑ evaluation process

The new attorney must have this information to fully understand the job expectations.[9] The new attorney may want to negotiate on some of the issues. At the end of the negotiation, hopefully the candidate will accept the position. Keep a list of "runner-up" candidates in order of preference, in case the first candidate turns down the offer and/or you

*Have a plan in place to orient and introduce the new attorney to other office staff.*

are unable to negotiate a satisfactory agreement. Once a candidate accepts the position, mail letters promptly to candidates who were not chosen.

### *Confirm the Offer*

Check with your human resources department about placing the offer in writing. Various offices handle this issue differently. Many send a confirmation letter after the candidate has verbally accepted the offer. The confirmation letter should contain the new attorney's salary, a description of the job duties and a start date.

### Start Off on the Right Foot

On the start date, assign an attorney to greet the new attorney and make him or her feel welcome. If new staff are left alone, they may feel ignored. Make them a part of the team right away.

Training should begin on the attorney's first day. The initial training may just be observation or court accompaniment, but some activity should be planned.

## CONCLUSION

So you decided to do the right thing and find the best candidate for the position. While following this procedure may not be simple or quick, it will increase the likelihood that your new attorney will be someone with the desired qualities. Representing a child welfare agency is hard. It is worth the extra effort to find someone who can live up to the challenge.

## ENDNOTES

1. "How to Form Hiring Teams." *Personnel Journal*, supplement August 1994, 14.

2. Keeva, Steven. "Opening the Mind's Eye." *ABA Journal*, June 1996, 48-56. *See generally*, Howze, Karen Aileen. *Making Differences Work*. Washington D.C.: American Bar Association, 1996.

3. Dietel, J. Edwin. "Hiring, Training, Evaluating, Compensating and Motivating Attorneys in the Government Law Department." *Federal Bar News & Journal* 34 (7), 1987, 318.

4. Based on American Bar Association CEELI Program. *Interviewing Skills Training: Selecting the Right Candidate.* Washington D.C.: ABA CEELI Program, 1998, Section I, 1.

5. Ibid at Section I, 4.

6. Ibid at Section I, 4-7; Coastal Human Resources. *Interviewing: Getting Beyond the Image.* Virginia Beach: Coastal Training Technologies Corp., 1996, 9-11.

7. Coastal Human Resources. *Legal and Effective Interviewing.* Virginia Beach: Coastal Training Technologies Corp., 1996, 14.

8. Author unknown. *Reference Checking.*

9. Debra Ratterman. "Guidelines for New Child Welfare Attorneys." *ABA Juvenile & Child Welfare Law Reporter* 10, July 1991, 78-79.

CHAPTER 3:

# A Guide to Retaining Agency Attorneys

Need to know how to keep a staff of agency attorneys on their feet and happy so they will stay a while? Start by putting yourself in their shoes. What do you need to do your job well? What barriers need to come down to promote top performance? What needs to happen for you to stay in your job long term?

This chapter gives agency attorney supervisors and staff tips on creating an environment in which attorneys give their best, feel content and committed, and, most importantly, want to stay.

## HOW TO KEEP AGENCY ATTORNEYS

Sit down with your staff and develop a list of factors that contribute to job satisfaction (see next page). Determine if your office provides these things. As a group, the staff can discuss what is and is not working and whether additional factors or ideas could be put in place to improve the office.

Additionally, there are certain needs that new attorneys have that should be addressed and certain guidelines that could be followed to retain more seasoned attorneys.

### 1. Welcome the new attorney

Welcome new attorneys and help them become a part of the office team as early as possible. If they feel positive, they will be more productive, willing to help their new colleagues, and become an integral

## Reasons Attorneys Remain in a Job

There are many reasons an attorney remains in a job. Managers need to consider these reasons when deciding how to create a positive work world. Here are some to think about:

- is offered financial incentives
- feels job is important/worthwhile/socially redeeming
- has set mutually acceptable goals with supervisor
- is able to meet the goals
- feels challenged yet not overburdened
- feels as if his or her skills are used effectively
- receives recognition for a job well done
- receives assistance from supervisors when necessary
- feels respected and supported
- believes a fair evaluation system is in place and is used

part of the staff. Consider the following when planning for a new attorney's arrival:

***No Floundering:*** Take new attorneys to court or meetings. Have written materials ready for them to read. Introduce them to their new colleagues. Have the office head explain the office's mission. Keep them busy, but try not to overwhelm them. Despite the very busy schedules of everyone in the office, new attorneys must not be left on their own in the first few days.

***Meaningful Mentoring:*** Some supervisory system must be in place. For example, a more experienced attorney can provide 1:1 attention for the new attorney. Mentoring has several benefits:

- ❑ The new attorney knows who to go to with direct questions.
- ❑ Court preparation will be consistent and thorough.
- ❑ The new attorney has an immediate contact.
- ❑ The supervising attorneys get new responsibility and some positive reinforcement for their developed skills.

The only potential drawback is that other responsibilities will need to be taken from the supervising attorney.

***Accessible Backup:*** In addition to having a mentor, the new attorney should know that colleagues can and will provide backup should the new attorney become overwhelmed or need assistance with a particularly difficult case or issue.

While every attorney in the office has a full schedule, it is important to bring the new attorney along slowly. Even if the new attorney has a lot of experience, adjusting to the new environment and learning how things are done can be difficult. If the new attorney feels supported, he or she will be more likely to help colleagues in return.

### 2. Appreciate the seasoned attorney

Just as it is important to be mindful of the new attorney's needs, seasoned attorneys need ongoing attention too. As an attorney has been at the office for a period of time, the caseworkers begin to trust the attorney and are more prone to seek the attorney's advice and follow it. Additionally, a seasoned attorney generally makes a stronger advocate for the client. Keep in mind that seasoned attorneys need:

***Positive Words:*** This may seem obvious, but employees are rarely told when they are doing well. Often, the attorney only hears when the agency or caseworker is angry. It is imperative to give positive reinforcement to let people know when they are doing well. It can be in many forms — letters, a kind word in passing, or an announcement in a staff meeting about an accomplishment.

***Pet Projects and Added Responsibility:*** Even though attorneys representing agencies are generally overloaded, sometimes special projects arise that draw on attorneys' particular interests. If so, give the attorney the opportunity to work on this project. An attorney's practice stays fresh and interesting if there are new areas to think about. Instead of randomly assigning these projects, approach

*Just as it is important to be mindful of the new attorney's needs, seasoned attorneys need ongoing attention too.*

attorneys who have expressed interest in new challenges or particular topics.

Similarly, it is a vote of confidence to make a seasoned attorney a supervisor. Also ask your experienced attorneys to conduct trainings for the agency or help implement new policies and practice reforms. Encourage them to sit on inter-agency task forces or court advisory boards. Draw public attention to their work by nominating them for community honors. With new responsibility comes respect from colleagues and members of the child welfare community, which can only make the seasoned attorney better.

Attorneys may complain they have too much to do. Sometimes their old tasks can be reassigned to accommodate the attorney who is taking on new challenges, but it is important for the attorney to continue to grow and learn.

***Pay Increases:*** While agency attorneys, as well as almost all attorneys in the child welfare field, are dedicated to improving the lives of children, *it is a job* and people need financial stability. Regular salary increases obviously are necessary financially, but also help boost the attorney's morale.

***Parties:*** Another way to improve morale is to provide staff with some fun activities where they can laugh and blow off steam. Arrange a potluck lunch, happy hour, or just a low key staff meeting where everyone can relax.

### 3. Trainings for all attorneys

Set aside time for group training, lectures, conferences, and recent case law and case reviews. No matter how long you've practiced, there is always more to learn and new developments that might improve your practice.

Additionally, attorneys in the office may have areas of expertise they could share with the group. The audience would learn new material and the presenter would gain valuable experience. Arrange a regular speaker series where local professionals and experts talk about their areas of interest. Expect that attorneys should and actually do attend conferences, and then share the information with their colleagues.

Sadly, training often becomes a low priority when work gets busy, however, it helps keep attorneys fresh and productive and must be emphasized to best serve the agency.

Suggested areas for trainings:

- ❑ We don't speak the same language or how to communicate with caseworkers/social workers
- ❑ Community services — what's available?
- ❑ Using expert witnesses in child abuse cases (include doctors, teachers, counselors and medical examiners)
- ❑ State appellate practice — what do we need to know?
- ❑ New law updates — how should cases be used in court?

*Pay Increases: While agency attorneys, as well as almost all attorneys in the child welfare field, are dedicated to improving the lives of children, it is a job and people need financial stability. Regular salary increases obviously are necessary financially, but also help boost the attorney's morale.*

- ❑ Agency policy — how is it formulated and applied?
- ❑ ASFA and permanency planning—what does it mean to us?
- ❑ Issues arising when parents or children suffer from mental health concerns, mental retardation and drug and alcohol dependence
- ❑ Managed care and its impact on the foster care system — what is "medical necessity" anyway?
- ❑ Education issues — what is the IDEA and how are foster children affected?
- ❑ Speaking with children — preparation for court in their language
- ❑ Principles of developmental psychology — how is that relevant?
- ❑ Domestic violence and its impact on children
- ❑ Negotiation techniques and when to use them

Challenge attorneys by encouraging them to take advantage of training opportunities and discussions about important legal issues.[1] A well-trained attorney enters the important negotiation, meeting or court hearing with confidence and therefore provides the best possible representation.

### 4. Maximize resources available to attorneys

***Support Staff:*** Attorneys need competent support staff and functioning equipment to produce quality work products and keep from burning out. Hire high quality legal assistants, legal interns, volunteer attorneys, secretarial and other support staff to ease some of the attorneys' workload.

Legal assistants can draft petitions, review files, send subpoenas, prepare exhibits, interview witnesses, do legal research and more.[2] A legal assistant or intern can also establish a resource library that is accessible and easy to use. The library should include statutes and regulations that control in your jurisdiction as well as publications, law reporters and journals concerning children and families. If these materials are on-site and organized, the attorneys may be more likely to spend time reading and educating themselves. The attorney will also have resources to write better motions, memorandums and briefs. For more information see chapter seven.

***Equipment:*** When the copy machine is constantly broken or the computer crashes once a week, the agency attorney is unable to concentrate on work for the client. This can frustrate the attorney and lead to dissatisfaction about the work environment. Make sure agency attorneys have operating fax machines, copy machines, office supplies, voice mail and individual computers with e-mail so they can best serve their client and stay satisfied in their positions.

***Staffing:*** Finally, the managing attorney or the agency administrator should hire a large enough staff to handle the work effectively and without regular staff burnout.[3] The office manager should learn about available grants to offset office costs and free money for staff. Additionally, federal money is available through Title IV-E matching funds. The manager must learn about the possibility of obtaining this money to increase the staff size.[4] If the attorneys and other staff members feel that they are being supported by the head of the office, they may work harder and truly serve the client.

## CONCLUSION

To provide the child welfare agency the best possible representation, attorneys must be treated well and trained to do their jobs. Generally, law school does not prepare a person for work in the child welfare system. Therefore, the attorneys must learn, from an interdisciplinary model, many things beyond simple trial skills. By respecting staff, improving their work environment and teaching them on an ongoing basis, the agency will benefit and, therefore, children will as well.

## ENDNOTES

1. Herring, David J. "Interdisciplinary Training and Assessing Community Services Resources." In *Agency Attorney Training Manual: Achieving Timely Permanency for Children by Implementing the Private Model of Legal Representation for the State Agency in Child Abuse and Neglect Matters.* Pittsburgh: University of Pittsburgh Law School, 1992; Dietel, J. Edwin. "Hiring, Training, Evaluating, Compensating and Motivating Attorneys in the Government Law Department." *Federal Bar News & Journal* 34(7), 1987, at 319.

2. Garcia, Mike Jay. "Key Trends in the Legal Profession." *Florida Bar Journal,* May 1997, 19-20.

3. Chiancone, Janet. "Representing the Child Welfare Agency: Establishing Caseload Standards." *ABA Child Law Practice*, 17(3), May 1998, 33, 38-40.

4. Segal, Ellen C. *Evaluating and Improving Child Welfare Agency Legal Representation Self Assessment Instrument and Commentary*. Washington, D.C.: ABA National Legal Resource Center for Child Advocacy and Protection, 1988, 58-61.

CHAPTER 4:

# Getting the Most from Performance Evaluations

## TWO LAWYERS, TWO VERY DIFFERENT EXPERIENCES. WHO WOULD YOU PREFER TO BE?

### Amy:

Amy has been an agency attorney for three years. She has been supervised by four different attorneys and has never had an official performance review. Over the years, she has asked for feedback about her progress in the office, but she has never been satisfied with the answers. She fears she has not made a lot of progress in her job over the past few years.

Amy just got a new boss, Margaret, who decided that an evaluation process was important. On her own, Margaret created an evaluation form and had the supervisors fill it out. She then called Amy into her office, handed her the evaluation and a summarizing paragraph and sent Amy on her way.

### Gina:

Gina has also been an agency attorney for three years, but she has had two supervisors over the years. Six months after she arrived, the chief of her unit, Susan, conducted an initial evaluation with Gina. The two sat down and discussed each of their goals for Gina. Additionally, they set out a system of supervision and training for the upcoming six months.

Since that time, Gina has participated in three annual reviews, during which her supervisors do a written evaluation of, among other things, her court performance, her interaction with her client and her written work. Gina fills out a brief self-evaluation. Then, Gina and Susan meet in a quiet conference room and discuss the positives and negatives of the evaluations. They also talk about goals for the next year. As the meeting ends, Susan always encourages Gina to see her if other questions or concerns arise.

In between the annual reviews, Gina's supervisor regularly checks in with Gina and offers positive and constructive criticism when appropriate.

Who would you rather be, Amy or Gina? Would you rather be the managing attorney running Amy's office or Gina's? Which office provides better support to its attorneys and therefore better representation to its client and ultimately to the children in the system?

Many offices around the country lack an adequate review process or have one that could be improved. Often, more senior attorneys feel like they did just fine without evaluations and newer attorneys will be fine if they keep working hard. By following some of the suggestions in this chapter, you can design a system that works for you and your attorneys, alleviate some frustration, include your

*If how children are served is the focus of the evaluation process, evaluations will be a useful tool rather than something the staff dreads.*

senior attorneys in the planning, and improve your office's practice.

## WHY THOROUGH, SUBSTANTIVE EVALUATIONS ARE NEEDED

### Importance for Children:

Agency attorneys are generally charged with filing abuse and neglect and termination of parental rights petitions. They are often responsible for trying court cases — bringing in witnesses, examining those witnesses, preparing exhibits, and all other aspects of a trial. Sometimes, they participate in mediations and pre-trial conferences. They make recommendations concerning foster care placement, visitation and adoption. While performing all of these tasks, they directly impact children. It is essential that they are trained, supervised and evaluated thoroughly.

Many attorneys in child welfare enter the field because they want to make a difference for the children in the system. To stay motivated and improve performance, attorneys need ongoing feedback, support and guidance on how their work serves children. If how children are served is the focus of the evaluation process, evaluations will be a useful tool rather than something the staff dreads.

To design a process that will improve the staff attorneys' skills and ultimately help children, consider some of the following questions:

- ❑ Are cases being moved to permanency in a timely manner?[1]
- ❑ Are attorneys taking advantage of training opportunities?
- ❑ Are their trial skills improving?
- ❑ Are they taking appeals that will improve a child's life?

If you consider these and other questions during the performance reviews, the job that you and your staff are doing for children will certainly improve.

### Importance for the Attorney:

There is not a person anywhere, in any position, who could not improve his or her job performance in some way. This is certainly true in a job that is stressful and complicated such as an agency attorney position. To make matters more difficult, many agency attorneys are, at least when they begin, new to the field and recent law school graduates.

Generally, they did not learn a lot about child welfare law in school. It is especially important for them that a good evaluation system be in place.

By having a fair and thorough evaluation system with clearly defined goals, the attorney will understand what is expected and will be able to track progress between evaluations. It is unreasonable to fault an attorney for not living up to particular standards if the attorney is not informed of those standards. Through constructive criticism the attorney can learn and improve in a supportive atmosphere.

### Importance for the Group:

The staff as a whole has a great deal to gain from a positive evaluation process. The staff should be involved in designing the system. This way, the evaluation will reflect their concerns. Including their input fosters loyalty to the office, "buy in" to the process and boosts morale.[2]

The benefits of having a consistent evaluation format for all attorneys are to:

- ***Uncover training needs.***[3] For instance, if many of the attorneys' evaluations demonstrate a weakness in examining expert witnesses, consider having a workshop on that topic.

- ❑ ***Identify weaknesses in the management of the office.*** For example, the evaluations may show that many attorneys were doing a poor job preparing for trial. You might want to have a staff meeting to discuss the reasons behind this. If it is because the attorneys do not have adequate time to prepare, or are in court every day in a week, consider looking at how staff are scheduled and whether there are enough attorneys to do the job that is expected.
- ❑ ***Identify attorneys' strengths.*** Using this information, consider restructuring how tasks are divided within the office to make better use of your staff. For instance, if you learn one attorney enjoys research and is skilled at it, you might decrease that attorney's court schedule and have him or her work on all of the appeals for the office. That person could also research new areas of the law and share the information with the other attorneys.
- ❑ ***Determine when an attorney is not performing at an acceptable level.*** You should meet with that person and help them decide whether he or she is on a good career path. If after that meeting, you believe the attorney does not want to leave, but that you can not help him or her improve enough, that attorney may need to be let go.

## FACTORS TO BE EVALUATED

When designing the evaluation process, you and your staff attorneys should first decide what aspects of the job and what attorney qualities you want to review. Discuss the values that you as a staff share and make sure the evaluation reflects those values.[4] Focus on the representation of the agency and the direct impact you have on children and families. Pick factors that can be measured and are written in language that all parties taking part in the process interpret in the same way.[5] Some of the factors may be accompanied by definitions.

Breaking the evaluation into categories can help make the form easier to use. Consider including the following factors in your evaluation. You and your staff may decide that there are others more relevant to your practice.

### Legal Ability

- ❑ Understands relevant state and federal child welfare law.
- ❑ Applies the law appropriately.

*Court related work:*

- ❑ Prepares thoroughly for trial (the agency deserves the best possible representation so that it can assist children and families).
- ❑ Goes to court prepared.
- ❑ Does not regularly request continuances (continuances cause unnecessary delays for children).
- ❑ Demonstrates ability to examine witnesses.
- ❑ Respects judge and all parties.
- ❑ Understands when and how to use exhibits.
- ❑ Shows willingness to try tough cases (otherwise borderline cases linger and children cannot progress towards permanent situations).
- ❑ Helps agency move cases.

*Written work:*

- ❑ Writing is clear, concise and coherent.
- ❑ Research skills are thorough.
- ❑ Legal citations are used appropriately.
- ❑ Accurate format used in briefs and memoranda.
- ❑ Negotiation skills are well tuned and attorney uses them in appropriate cases (families often benefit by being "heard" in a non-courtroom setting).

*Appellate work:*

- ❑ Is open to appealing cases.
- ❑ Follows through on appeals.
- ❑ Writes thorough and effective appellate briefs.
- ❑ Delivers quality oral arguments.

### Case Management

- ❑ Is able to move cases in timely fashion (delays negatively affect children's chances at permanence).
- ❑ Files petitions in timely fashion.
- ❑ Prioritizes work appropriately.
- ❑ Delegates work when appropriate (an over-worked and over-stressed attorney cannot provide adequate representation).

### Delivery of Client Services

- ❑ Understands relationship with agency as client (confusion about the relationship impairs ability to adequately represent the client).
- ❑ Inspires client confidence (trust is essential to quality representation).
- ❑ Respects caseworkers and all agency staff.
- ❑ Demonstrates ability to counsel client.

### Teamwork and Leadership

- ❑ Is motivated (a high energy level and strong commitment are needed to get good results for children and families).
- ❑ Is able to motivate others.
- ❑ Is able to work as a team (being involved in abused children's lives can be emotionally difficult; sharing work and support with colleagues is important to prevent burnout).
- ❑ Delegates tasks when appropriate.
- ❑ Responsive to constructive criticism.
- ❑ Effectively supervises others (if applicable).

### Attitude and Personal Qualities

- ❑ Is creative problem solver (child abuse cases are rarely clear cut – by looking at them from different angles you can come up with innovative solutions).
- ❑ Knows when to ask questions and asks them.
- ❑ Takes risks when appropriate.
- ❑ Interacts with others in nonjudgmental manner.
- ❑ Takes initiative.
- ❑ Is enthusiastic about the field and the job.
- ❑ Understands boundaries — does not get too personally involved in cases.
- ❑ Gives priority to improving the lives of children and families.[6]

## STRIVE FOR ACCOUNTABILITY — WAYS TO EVALUATE THE FACTORS

Information about the attorney will not just come to you, you will need to gather it. You should try to obtain information that is concrete and measurable. These methods may include:

- ❑ ***Court Observation*** — go to court and observe the attorney. How affective are the attorney's trial skills? Is the attorney moving cases or requesting many continuances?
- ❑ ***File Reviews*** — Is the attorney submitting written motions to the court? Are petitions being filed in a timely manner?
- ❑ ***Discussion with Colleagues*** — Talking to some of the people at the agency or in court can help determine how the attorney handles him or herself, whether cases on the attorney's caseload are moving forward in a timely fashion and whether the attorney is willing to take risks and try difficult cases. It is easier to measure these qualities if the attorneys handle a case from beginning to end.

Remember that when working in the court system, many things such as moving a case may be out of the attorney's control. However, you and your staff should be trying to do as much as possible within the system's constraints. The attorneys should be accountable for the things that are in their control — e.g., filing petitions and being prepared to move forward on the day of trial.

### Factors Not to Over Emphasize

Often, attorneys are so focused on case statistics that quality of representation is overlooked. If an attorney believes that winning all cases is the most

*While winning a case is obviously more fun and better than losing it, evaluating the win/loss record of your staff attorneys is not as important as evaluating their skills.*

important factor, there could be a temptation to only try clear-cut cases. This would not benefit enough of the children in the agency's custody.

There are, for example, termination of parental rights cases that are difficult because the parent has done some of what was expected, but not nearly enough to care for the child. If it is in that child's best interest to be adopted, the agency attorney has the responsibility to file the petition, be prepared for a tough hearing, and try as hard as possible to terminate the parent's rights. If the judge rules in the parent's favor, the attorney should be praised for his or her efforts and supported so that the attorney does not become discouraged. You might also encourage the attorney to appeal the case.

### Structuring the Evaluation Process

In addition to discussing the factors to be evaluated with your staff, you should design the entire process with them. If you have a large staff, you may want a committee of volunteers to work on this project. After the process is designed but before it is implemented, have a meeting with the entire staff to explain your goals and the evaluation system.

Some issues you should consider and questions you should answer when designing the evaluation include:

## THE EVALUATION ITSELF

### Will there be a self-evaluation component?

A self-evaluation can help the attorney focus on his or her own strengths, weaknesses, accomplishments in the prior year and goals for the upcoming year. It is also a way for the attorney to prepare for meetings with supervisors about the evaluation. However, agency attorneys are busy people who may not want to spend time filling out another form. The self-evaluation, if you choose to use it, must be short and it needs to serve a specific purpose. The attorneys should know why they are doing it and how it will fit into the overall evaluation process.

### What will the evaluation form look like?

The evaluation form should be easy to follow and understand. Consider what type of rating scale to use, if any. Most rating scales are either one to three or one to five. Discuss these or other scales and their benefits and drawbacks with the committee. Your scale could resemble one of the following examples:

| | |
|---|---|
| **E** — Exceeds Standards<br>**M** —Meets Standards<br>**B** — Below Standards / Needs Improvement | **NO** — Not Observed<br>**NI** — Needs Improvement<br>**AP** — Acceptable Performance<br>**SP** — Superior Performance[7] |
| **1** — Outstanding<br>**2** — Exceeds Standards<br>**3** — Meets Standards<br>**4** — Below Standards<br>**5** — Seriously Deficient | |

The form should also have space for narrative comments. The comments should be concrete and emphasize examples of the attorney's behavior. The comments could also focus on goals and areas for improvement as well as obstacles the attorney has overcome in the prior year. The comments should also be as positively worded as possible and if they include criticism they should offer steps to overcome the problems.

### Who should fill out the evaluation?

Everyone who directly supervises the attorney should complete the evaluation form. As the managing attorney, even if you are not the staff attorney's direct supervisor, you should also consider doing an evaluation. By completing one yourself you will focus on what you know and perhaps what you feel you should know about the attorney's performance and progress in the office.

### Will there be an explanation and instructions attached to the evaluation form and who will write them?

Instructions should address the goals of the evaluation process, the values that you are attempting to address and the steps that each participant should take to complete their part of the process. Perhaps a subset of your committee could write the instructions and get approval from the committee. You as the managing attorney will have ultimate discretion.

### Will there be a definition section to explain each factor, and who will write that?

There should also be a definition section so that anyone working with the evaluation will understand the criteria. Again, a subset of the committee could work on it.[8]

## FEEDBACK AND THE EVALUATION INTERVIEW

### What is the purpose of the interview?

The interview following the evaluation is a very important part of the process. It is during this interview that you can talk with the staff attorney about the positives and negatives of the evaluation and most importantly set goals for the upcoming year.

### Structuring the interview

Before the meeting you and the staff attorney should agree on a convenient time to meet. Find a quiet room where you won't be interrupted. Both of you should take the time before the meeting to prepare. You should review all of the evaluations about this attorney and think about what you hope to communicate during the interview.

During the meeting there should be a two-way conversation. If you used self-evaluations, the staff attorney could talk about it. What did the attorney feel he or she accomplished in the prior year and what is the attorney looking forward to in the upcoming year? How have the attorney's accomplishments benefited the children and families served?

Review the evaluations with the attorney and discuss with the attorney any barriers that he or she may see to improving in the job. Then, together, discuss goals. It is important that the attorney leave the meeting with a clear sense of what you expect in the upcoming year. At the end, summarize the meeting and ask if the attorney has any questions or concerns.[9]

### Will the supervisor change anything in the evaluation as a result of the meeting?

This is a topic that your committee should discuss and that you will need to make a final decision about. Feedback and dialogue are necessary in this process especially to guide the attorney towards progress. However, managers have different opinions about whether the employee's comments should influence the supervisor's evaluation. If you use self-evaluations, that form should be included in the packet that is placed in the attorney's personnel file. Additionally, you could make written notes about the substance of your meeting with the attorney and include any concerns that the attorney had about the evaluations.

**Will anyone other than supervisors give feedback about the employee?**

Consider eliciting feedback from people with whom the staff attorney regularly interacts. This could include someone from the agency, a judge, or some of the other attorneys the attorney works with in court. Give careful thought to how you elicit the comments, who you ask for the comments and how you want them incorporated in the evaluation process.

Remember to make the primary focus of the questions how the attorney's work impacts children and families in your system. Consider asking the

## TIPS FOR MANAGERS

Think about whether your office policy supports attorneys who take risks, even if they do not win. If it does not, consider reworking the policy and how it plays out.

- Include staff in developing and implementing the evaluation process.
- Provide constructive criticism and positive reinforcement.
- Use the evaluation system to identify training needs and develop a training program.
- Use the evaluation system to accentuate the strengths of the staff.

attorney if there is someone in particular he or she would want you to contact. While the comments could be helpful to assess how the attorney is interacting with others and how the client perceives the attorney, more weight should be given to supervisory evaluations.

### Will the evaluation process be connected with salary increases?

In most offices, annual salary increases are associated in some way with the evaluation process. Opinions differ on whether the connection should be made. At least in the initial meeting between you and the attorney, salary should not be a central focus. If money is part of the discussion, the main points of the interview — goal setting and improving practice — could be lost. When possible, you should schedule a follow up meeting to revisit any aspects of the first interview that were unresolved and discuss salary.[10]

Even when an agency attorney receives a salary increase it is generally not a substantial amount of money. For this reason, you may also want to consider nonmonetary incentives for attorneys who are doing well. Kind words or an appreciative card can go a long way towards making the attorney feel appreciated. Attorneys should be praised for achievements so that they feel encouraged and want to continue their good work.

## WHEN THE PROCESS IS COMPLETE

After the evaluation process is complete, give serious thought to its effectiveness. There are probably things that could be improved. Brainstorm with the attorneys who actually went through the process to come up with creative ways to make the evaluation more useful the next time around.

When new attorneys are hired, talk with them about the evaluation process and let them know what factors will be considered in their review. This will ensure that there are no unfair surprises at evaluation time.

Remember that evaluation and training should not be a once a year experience. Supervisors should work with newer attorneys throughout the year. Supervisors should regularly check in with the attorney to see if the attorney is handling the workload and pressure of the job. The supervisor could consistently assist the attorney with court preparation and observe court performance to really help the attorney grow in the position. When the attorney feels supported, he or she will perform better.

Review the evaluations as a whole with the goal of establishing a training program. If there are topics the staff would benefit from learning about, set up a training session. If there are individual attorneys who need assistance in certain areas, help them find legal education classes or conferences to attend. When they return, they could share their new knowledge with the entire staff.

## CONCLUSION

Designing and implementing an effective attorney evaluation process is a challenge, but one that is essential to improve agency attorneys' performance. If Amy had such a system in place, she would not have felt the frustration that she did. A thorough, organized, well-structured evaluation will support your attorneys, help them reach their potential in the job and keep them motivated. Most importantly, it will result in excellent attorneys who will be able to directly improve the lives of the children in your community.

## ENDNOTES


1. Laver, Mimi. "Implementing ASFA: A Challenge for Agency Attorneys." *Child Law Practice* 17(8), October 1998.

2. Matheson, Wayne, Cornelius Van Dyk, Kenneth Millar. *Performance Evaluation in the Human Services.* New York: The Hawthorn Press, 1995, 29-30.

3. Studley, Jamienne S. "Good or Bad, Evaluations are Critical." *Legal Times,* April 15, 1991, 14.

4. Armstrong, Michael. "Measuring Work: the Vital Statistics." *People Management* 21, September 1995, 34-35.

5. Matheson, 1995, 29.

6. Based on *Fair Measure: Toward Effective Attorney Evaluations.* Chicago: American Bar Association Commission on Women in the Profession, 1997, 56-59.

7. *Fair Measure,* 1997, 22-23, 70.

8. Ibid, 49-54.

9. Ibid, 108-109; Studley, 1991, 11, 14; Brown, Jerry and Denise Dudley. "How to Select, Train and Evaluate Employees." In *The Supervisor's Guide: The Everyday Guide to Coordinating People and Tasks.* Mission, Kansas: SkillPath Publications, 1989, 30-31.

10. Brown et al., 1989, 32.

CHAPTER 5:

# TEAMS WITHIN THE TEAM:

## SAN DIEGO COUNTY COUNSEL JUVENILE DEPENDENCY DIVISION

If management to an office could be both structured and flexible at the same time, you'd have the Juvenile Dependency Division (JDD) in San Diego. The JDD as a whole operates as a cohesive team. Within the JDD, staff is divided into five smaller teams. There are 21 legal and paralegal staff members in the unit. The structure provides opportunity for excellent supervision, evaluation, information sharing and as a result, top notch-representation for the San Diego County Health and Human Services Agency.

***This is how it works:***

## THE STRUCTURE

Susan Strom, the Chief Deputy County Counsel for the JDD, heads the unit. She supervises the entire staff, sits on many court committees, is the key contact person for the head of the agency and generally oversees the functioning of the office. For hands-on management, Susan relies on five team leaders.

To be a team leader, a person needs a minimum of four years of experience in juvenile dependency law. When I met with the team leaders, I learned their experience in dependency law far exceeded the minimum: it ranged from 12 to 30 years in the field.

The teams consist of lawyers, paralegals, investigators and secretaries. In addition, there is one other team of legal-procedures clerks who maintain the file system, update case status on the computer system, keep statistics and type subpoenas.

Four teams are assigned to particular courtrooms: three teams are assigned to two courts each and one team covers one court and screening and discovery. The fifth team concentrates on appeals, writs, guardianship and other substantive issues. See chapter seven for more information about the appeals team and their resources.

The team leaders take their job as mentors very seriously. They consider attorney experience when assigning work. They accompany new attorneys to court and keep their doors open so the attorneys can ask questions. What makes the team structure workable for such a busy office is that the team leaders are open to advising nonteam members as well. Several attorneys told me they always know which person to go to with questions. If their team leader is unavailable, the others are always willing to help. Additionally, team members are constantly helping each other out.

In addition to assigning work, mentoring, appearing in court or writing briefs themselves, and conducting trainings for the agency, team leaders are primarily responsible for evaluating the members of their teams.

## HIRING

The JDD has low turnover. When they do need to hire, however, there is a clear procedure in place. There are two steps in the process. After the ad is placed, the office receives about 100 resumes. The human relations staff of the county counsel office does the initial paper screen. When that is completed, either the team leaders or Susan and one team leader do the interviews.

A job description exists for all positions. According to Susan, applicants must be empathetic, able to work in a team (no loners), have a sense of professionalism, and be able to communicate well. Susan looks for individuals who have knowledge of dependency law, strong academics and field experience. In the past, Susan has hired a number of former interns because they are familiar with the unit's work. Currently the staff has an attorney who used to be a social worker in San Diego County.

The JDD hires career track staff, so no one is placed in the unit against their will. Therefore, when hiring, Susan tries hard to find people who will fit into the team setting.

## EVALUATIONS

About two years ago, the San Diego County Counsel office began an evaluation process. Each unit has its own format with emphasis on the most important aspect of the unit's jobs. While most people said it was a time-consuming process, they also commented that it was a good experience and positive learning tool.

The team leaders fill out evaluations for each team member; Susan then works with the team leaders to finalize them. Each attorney does a self-evaluation focusing on past year accomplishments and upcoming goals.

*Additionally, a Client Satisfaction Survey is sent to the agency about each attorney. The results have been extremely positive.*

After the written pieces are completed, the team leader meets with each attorney to discuss the outcome. Several attorneys told me their team leaders meet with them regularly to raise issues and give positive feedback. During the evaluation process, therefore, there are few surprises.

The evaluation is broken into three main categories: Overall Performance Rating, Goals and Objectives, and Ratings of Performance Functions. The latter is further broken into:

- ❑ delivery of legal services
- ❑ risk identification and mitigation
- ❑ client relations
- ❑ teamwork/collaboration
- ❑ administrative skills and responsibility
- ❑ supervision responsibilities

Each category is then further divided into individual elements.

Performance standards for each topic have been developed and distributed to all attorneys. This way, the evaluator has objective factors on which to base the evaluation. See Appendix C for the evaluation and performance standards.

### Morale Building

The entire staff of the JDD appeared to be positive about the office and their colleagues. I asked what the office does to keep morale positive in the high stress environment. I heard about team lunches, potlucks including an annual barbecue, baby showers, group trips to ball games and a County

*First, everyone makes a big deal the first day a new staff member joins the JDD.*

Counsel softball team. Two activities made a particular impression.

For one attorney there was a reception with a cake; she was provided with a manual and things to do from the beginning.[1] The second thing is that colleagues are supportive of each other in tough times as well as good. When family emergencies hit, people step in for one another and do what they can to pull together.[2]

## CONCLUSION

In the JDD there are teams within the larger unit; these teams are made up of individuals who thrive on support, training, mentoring and feedback about their performance. As a result of the attention to both the individual and the team, the unit functions as a cohesive body providing high level representation to the agency. The agency staff believe the representation they receive is very good and attorneys are attentive to their needs.[3] Focusing on JDD staff, then, results in good outcomes for the agency and therefore the children and families of San Diego.[4]

### ENDNOTES

1. Interview with Katherine Bird, Deputy County Counsel, March 11, 1999.

2. Interview with John Phillips, Deputy Cunty Counsel and Team Leader, March 11, 1999.

3. Interview with Yvonne Campbell, Deputy Director, Health and Human Services Agency of San Diego County, March 12, 1999.

4. This chapter was based on interviews with and observations of the attorneys and staff of the San Diego County Counsel, Juvenile Dependency Division, March 11-12, 1999.

CHAPTER 6:

# Representing the Child Welfare Agency:

ESTABLISHING CASELOAD STANDARDS

by Janet Chiancone & Mark Hardin

## ARE YOU OVERWHELMED WITH CASES?

**Take a quick test:**

- ❑ Do you spend more than half your time in court?
- ❑ Do you receive over 50 new cases in a year?

If you answered yes to either of these questions, chances are your caseloads are far too high.

High caseloads tend to be the norm rather than the exception for those working in the child welfare field. Even though child welfare agencies have established caseload standards for their caseworkers,

### Attorney Workload

**"Attorney workload can significantly affect the quality of representation...A caseload of 40 to 50 active child welfare cases (abuse/neglect adjudications, TPRs, and appeals) appears to be a reasonable size, fewer than 40 is preferable, and an average caseload of over 60 seems to be unmanageable."**

Source: Segal, E. C. *Evaluating and Improving Child Welfare Agency Legal Representation: Self Assessment Instrument and Commentary.* Washington, D.C.: ABA National Legal Resource Center for Child Advocacy and Protection, 1990, 17.

in most cases their attorneys continue to be assigned an overwhelming number of cases. In some jurisdictions it is not uncommon for a single child welfare attorney to handle over 200 cases a year.

Since many offices have minimal support, attorneys also perform administrative duties, adding to their workloads. With the new timelines and requirements of the *Adoption and Safe Families Act of 1997*,[1] agency attorneys' workloads may greatly increase. Establishing caseload standards provides agencies and lawmakers with a concrete justification for hiring more attorneys.

### Why Caseload Standards Are So Important

High caseloads comprise the safety and well-being of children by extending the time they stay in "foster care limbo" waiting for permanency. Research on the impact of high caseloads on attorneys' performance in general can also be applied to attorneys representing child welfare agencies. The research finds high caseloads can impact:

- ❑ ***The quality of representation.*** One study of attorneys in juvenile court found high caseloads were the "single most important barrier to effective representation."[2] The high caseloads often made it very difficult for attorneys to: meet with clients, conduct a thorough investigation, research and write individualized pretrial documents, keep informed about community based programs, and follow up with clients after proceedings.[3]
- ❑ ***Burnout and turnover among lawyers.***[4] Attorneys with high caseloads are at much higher risk of burnout. The study described above found most lawyers with caseloads between 200 and 500 stayed in their jobs less than two years.[5]

## Responsibilities Reported By Agency Attorneys*

In addition to litigation and case preparation, several attorneys recently interviewed by the ABA Center on Children and the Law report the following responsibilities:

- consulting with CPS workers on whether to accept a case
- filing petitions
- providing training (to social workers and other attorneys)
- trial and calendar preparation
- filing appeals
- attending community meetings
- legal research
- administrative work (typing, filing)
- communicating with the public on highly-publicized cases

While we may think of agency attorneys as being responsible for representing the child welfare agency in abuse and neglect cases, other tasks they report include:

- developing agency policy
- writing regulations
- administrative hearings
- juvenile delinquency cases
- adult protective services cases
- employee termination cases

**Based on interviews with agency attorneys in California, New Jersey, New Mexico, New Hampshire, Maryland and Pennsylvania.*

*High caseloads compromise the safety and well-being of children by extending the time they stay in "foster care limbo" waiting for permanency.*

"The intense emotional nature of child-related litigation must be considered. Especially if an advocate does not have a diversified caseload, the stresses inherent in a child advocacy practice are immense. An attorney with a high caseload will be bombarded with case after case of family dysfunction."[6] High caseloads make managing the workload nearly impossible, resulting in job dissatisfaction and "anxiety over never having enough time to do a complete job."[7] Coupled with inadequate training, high turnover and a lack of administrative support services, it is little wonder that burnout levels are so high.[8]

- ❑ ***The risk of professional conduct violations and malpractice claims***. "The vast majority of grievances and malpractice claims [against attorneys] are the result of some kind of administrative error,"[9] often as a result of having too many cases to handle. A lack of communication with clients is also often a key issue. Of the approximately 6,500 misconduct charges filed against attorneys in one state (Illinois), nearly 1,500 resulted from neglect or lack of communication.[10]

### Cover the Basics

To establish caseloads, some basic standards and procedures should be in place At a minimum, however, your office should:

- ❑ ***Establish guidelines for the specific responsibilities and tasks of agency attorneys in your jurisdiction.*** Is there a job description for the position? Is it the same as other public attorneys or are there specific tasks outlined? Do guidelines include both litigation and nonlitigation responsibilities?
- ❑ ***Focus on establishing good office procedures.*** Is the office equipped with modern technology (computers, fax machines, e-mail)? Are attorneys computer literate? What type of office support is available (secretaries, paralegals)? Is there a system in place to help attorneys track filing deadlines, court dates, and monitor case progress?
- ❑ ***Streamline and standardize routine tasks performed by attorneys.***[11] Are there "boiler plate" materials (e.g., relevant petitions, motions, court orders) available for attorneys to adapt? Is there a checklist to be used when preparing cases for trial?

### Caseload Considerations

Regardless of the method you use to assess your office's caseload needs, consider the following:

- ❑ ***Define the case.*** What is a case? A single child or family? Are termination of parental rights (TPRs) considered separate cases? What about appeals?
- ❑ ***Does the same attorney handle the case through all proceedings?*** Resource Guidelines endorsed by the ABA strongly advocate a practice of case continuity in representation.[12] Do all attorneys handle TPRs, or are they handled by a different set of attorneys? How is case continuity assured in these cases? Case continuity makes

## Basic Steps in Conducting A Caseload Assessment

- Select the appropriate individual to lead the effort. An attorney who has worked in the office for several years is probably the best person to conduct an assessment. Someone who has good organizational and analytical skills, and who is comfortable consulting with other staff members.
- Include all agency legal staff in the workload assessment. This includes supervisors, attorneys, paralegals, and other support staff.
- Encourage honesty in the assessment. Reassure agency staff that all experiences are needed in order to get a complete picture. Each case and each attorney is unique, and information about the range of experiences is needed to formulate the "typical" case.
- Gain access to basic agency statistics for the past few years. The number of petitions filed, number of TPRs and other agency statistics are needed to provide a complete picture of the agency's history and future.
- Be aware of any new or pending legislation that might affect future practice. For example, the new federal *Adoption and Safe Families Act of 1997* requires a permanency planning hearing within 12 months of disposition, and initiation of TPR proceedings within 15 months, subject to certain exceptions. Keep this in mind as you determine the number of cases that typically result in a TPR. The numbers may increase in future years due to this new law. Changes in state law may also affect future practice.

attorneys more accountable and the process more efficient.[13]

- **_Account for all responsibilities of an agency attorney._** In addition to court time and court preparation, attorneys may be involved in training, screening and other duties. See the box on page 6-83 for a list of responsibilities reported by agency attorneys.
- **_Plan enough time for case preparation._** A good ratio for prep time to court time is 3:1.[14] One agency attorney reported frustration at never having enough time to meet with other attorneys and discuss proposed service plans. She noted that attorneys "need blocks of time outside of the courtroom so that agreed orders can be negotiated, when appropriate, to move cases along more quickly."[15]
- **_Consider the level of case difficulty._** One jurisdiction in Tennessee reports that TPRs are classified into three groups: simple/straightforward, complex, and very complex. These levels allow for better planning when allocating time and resources.
- **_Plan for travel time._** Travel time is a major planning consideration, especially in rural areas, where one or two attorneys cover a large area.
- **_Adjust caseloads for managing and new attorneys._** Managing attorneys often require a lower caseload so they can fulfill their supervisory responsibilities. In addition, new attorneys will likely need lower caseloads as they become acclimated to the work.

*A good ratio for prep time to court time is 3:1.*[14]

In addition to the above, the box on page 6-86 outlines some basic steps to help make sure your assessment is complete.

## CONCLUSION

Attorneys who represent the agency have a unique mission in child welfare. It is possible they play the most crucial role in moving cases through the court process and on to permanency. Yet, they are often overwhelmed with cases. Agencies should conduct an assessment to establish caseload standards that are workable for attorneys. In the end, this will help children achieve permanency sooner.

## ENDNOTES

1. P.L. 105-89

2. Puritz, P. et al. "Due Process Advocacy Project Report: Seeking Better Representation for Young Offenders." *Criminal Justice* 10, Winter 1996, 18.

3. Ibid.

4. Ibid.

5. Ibid.

6. Grasso, K.L. & H. Davidson. *A Judge's Guide To Improving The Legal Representation of Children.* Washington, D.C.: ABA Center on Children and the Law, 1998, 68.

7. Puritz, et. al., 1996, 18.

8. Ibid.

9. Gibeaut, J. "Avoiding Trouble at the Mill." *ABA Journal*, March 1997, 49.

10. Ibid.

11. Segal, E.C. *Evaluating and Improving Child Welfare Agency Legal Representation: Self Assessment Instrument and Commentary*. Washington, D.C.: American Bar Association National Legal Resource Center for Child Advocacy and Protection, 1990.

12. *Resource Guidelines: Improving Court Practice in Child Abuse & Neglect Cases*. Reno, NV: National Council of Juvenile and Family Court Judges, 1995.

13. Segal, 1990, 50.

14. Mark Hardin, ABA Center on Children and the Law, March 1998.

15. Anonymous (Interview with Agency Attorney, February 1998).

CHAPTER 7:

# MAKE LIFE EASIER: USING ALL OF YOUR RESOURCES WELL

Do you ever feel you are spinning your wheels? Replicating work that's already been done? Doing things that might not really be your job? Has your office made progress purchasing the "basics" in office supplies, but could use resources more effectively and make your work life easier?

This chapter highlights a few creative ways agency attorney offices are using resources. They include using paralegals effectively, networking computers, using Brief and Motions Banks and developing common forms. They might be worth adapting for your office.

## THE BASICS

Some essentials to running your office:

- ❑ abundant office supplies: paper, pens, case files, etc.
- ❑ office equipment that works: copy machines, fax, voice mail
- ❑ personal computers for word processing, e-mail and Internet access
- ❑ access to Westlaw or Lexis as well as a law library
- ❑ support staff with well-defined roles

The need for these things is clear, and it goes without saying that you should have them. The key to making your life easier is thinking of creative ways to acquire and use resources. For example, one thing you may not know is that your local Bar Association may be able to help purchase supplies and equipment at a reduced cost.[1] Additionally, there are ways to cut down on waste – using less paper, recycling supplies – that may make your basics last longer.

## BEYOND THE BASICS

Using your resources well saves time and allows you to focus on the lawyering aspects of your job. Many agency attorney offices throughout the country have found creative ways to make the most of what they have available. What follows are a few examples.

### Staffing

***Paralegals: Law Department of Philadelphia – Health and Human Services Unit***

My former office successfully uses legal assistants to help represent the Department of Human Services (DHS). The legal assistants are college-educated and many are also certified paralegals. They are hired for the unit and are therefore aware of the types of cases on which they will work. When hiring, the attorneys and legal assistant supervisors are careful to choose people who are comfortable with the emotional aspect of child abuse and neglect work.

The unit now has two legal assistant supervisors and eight legal assistants. Eight more legal assistants will soon be hired to join the team. The legal assistants are assigned to different areas.

One of the supervisors and three legal assistants (and eventually all eight new hires) are assigned to the Permanency Planning Initiative (PPI). PPI matches attorneys and legal assistants with caseworker units at DHS. As a specialized team, the caseworkers and legal staff work on the case from beginning through permanency. They strive to provide children permanency as quickly as possible. PPI legal assistants draft initial petitions and termination of parental rights petitions (TPR), attend *all* meetings on their cases, regularly communicate with the caseworkers, help attorneys prepare for trial, and conduct legal research. Because the attorneys spend much time in court, the legal assistant often helps the caseworkers understand what needs to be done on the cases.

Five legal assistants are assigned to the other DHS cases. Each day one of them is at DHS answering questions (and directing questions to the attorneys) and drafting initial petitions. They also draft TPR petitions by reviewing the DHS file and communicating with the caseworker to determine the relevant facts to include. They conduct legal research, subpoena witnesses and do other trial preparation work as needed. This group is supervised by a legal assistant supervisor who is also assigned to a new Court Improvement model court.

Philadelphia's Court Improvement model court is a new program in which one judge presides over dependency cases, from filing through permanency. Two child advocates, two city solicitors, and a few parents' attorneys handle all cases from filing to permanency. In each case, the parties meet for mediation before a hearing. Service providers are present to set up evaluations for the parties on the spot. The program provides intensive, upfront services to families to speed permanency for the children.

In model court, the legal assistant supervisor assigns court dates to new cases, manages case files, participates in pretrial conferences and mediation, drafts petitions for the cases, conducts some research, and participates in ASFA-related policy discussions.[2]

The legal assistants work closely with the unit's 20 attorneys, who review their work and answer any legal questions. Having a strong team of qualified legal assistants frees the attorneys to concentrate on their court cases, appeals, briefs and other tasks. Using legal assistants is more cost-effective than having attorneys do certain tasks and the teamwork provides a high level of representation for DHS.[3]

### Practice ideas

A few ideas about recruiting new legal assistants:

- ❑ Contact the placement office at local paralegal schools. For a list of these programs see the *Guide for Legal Assistant Education Programs*[4] (available for $10 through the ABA Customer Service Center: 800/285-2221 Order #: 423-003509-98). These programs may provide you with graduating legal assistants who need full time jobs, or interns who you could train and possibly hire when they graduate.
- ❑ Contact the ABA Standing Committee on Legal Assistants, 312/988-5616. Web site: ***www.abanet.org/legalassts/home.html***.
- ❑ Contact the National Association for Legal Assistants at 1516 S. Boston, #200, Tulsa, OK 74119, 918/587-6828. Web site: ***www.nala.org***. Provides information about continuing education

and paralegal certification programs, among other things.

- ❑ Contact the National Federation of Paralegal Associations (NFPA), P.O. Box 33108, Kansas City, MO 64114, 816/941-4000. Web site: ***www.paralegals.org***. Provides information about schools, membership and job listings. You may want to post your available position with NFPA.
- ❑ Check with your local or state bar associations to see if they have a committee on paralegals. If so, they may be able to steer you to paralegals interested in child welfare work.
- ❑ Create a job description so you and your prospective paralegals will be clear about the responsibilities of the person in the position. It could look something like:

*Under attorney supervision, the paralegal will be responsible for: meeting with caseworkers and drafting petitions; answering some caseworker questions and referring others to attorneys; drafting termination of parental rights petitions; subpoenaing witnesses; conducting trial preparation as needed by the attorneys; conducting legal research, interviewing witnesses; and participating in some policy questions as they relate to the position.*

### Support Staff: County Counsel of Santa Clara County – Child Dependency Unit

On a recent visit to California, I met with legal and nonlegal staff in the Child Dependency Unit (CDU). I was taken by the level of teamwork and camaraderie in the office, and the way the support staff was structured to help make the attorneys' jobs more manageable.

The Administrative Support Officer for the CDU supervises the 13 support staff; meets regularly with the lead attorneys and paralegal; serves as the safety officer (overseeing fire safety protocol and reporting accidents); handles any facility issues; oversees the upkeep of all equipment, the distribution of court reports and the supply purchases; and provides a support system for the staff she supervises.

The Administrative Support Officer told me that when she started in the CDU three years before, the unit had five copy machines, but none worked well. With persistence, she fought for higher quality machines, and now the unit only needs four copiers. She also oversees the purchase of supplies and is able to get the office what it needs. She is careful to keep extra copies of important forms in her office so the unit doesn't run out.[5]

The 13 support staff include three legal secretaries, each assigned to a team of attorneys and paralegals; five clerk typists, two of whom are responsible for all notice filings; three receptionists, two of whom staff the courthouse; and two file clerks.[6] These staff members bring many benefits to the office. For instance, I asked the attorneys why they had a receptionist rather than direct phone lines.

The receptionist provides a good first impression for outside callers. She directs callers to the correct attorneys and handles some problems herself. She always has a copy of the court calendar and can direct caseworkers to the attorney handling court on a given day. She saves attorneys time while making the approximately 150 callers-a-day feel like their questions were answered.[7]

The clerks also assist the legal staff a great deal. Two file clerks keep the file room in exceptional

*The receptionist provides a good first impression for outside callers.*

order. They maintain a filing system for open and closed cases, and the attorneys never have to worry about finding or spending time refiling a case.

Other support staff are in charge of distributing court reports. In Santa Clara County, the court requires the agency reports well before the hearing. The CDU support staff must be sure the caseworker delivers the reports to the CDU office and they send the reports to the appropriate parties and the court. The Administrative Support Officer helps resolve all logistical issues with this process. By performing this task, the attorneys and caseworkers are free to handle other matters.

The notice clerks send approximately 40,000 notice letters to parties and foster parents a year. Before the CDU took on this responsibility, notice letters were not sent consistently. Now, the task is done correctly, the agency's obligation is handled, and the attorneys do not need to worry about this issue.

These examples show how important it is to have someone on staff who is in charge of running the office. Because of the Administrative Support Officer's oversight and the support staff's efforts, the attorneys in the CDU do not worry about equipment breaking, parties not receiving notice, files getting lost, or supplies running low.

### Practice Ideas

Hiring more support staff would probably be ideal, however if you cannot do so, consider reallocating tasks to current staff. As in San Jose, it might be more efficient to assign particular jobs to each person, rather than everyone doing a piece of all jobs. For instance, one person may be kept busy with filing and that person could keep the file area orderly and accessible. If many people work on this, it may be more difficult to use.

There are several low-cost ways to increase your staff. Consider part-time or temporary attorneys, legal assistants or legal secretaries for particular projects or when you are in "crunch mode."[8] Also consider hiring law students as part time clerks.[9] Sometimes they will work for credit if you set it up with the local law school. One drawback is that students often need a lot of supervision and they typically only stay for a summer or semester. However, they can do research and work on discrete projects that your staff may not have time to address.

## Technology

### *Brief Banks and other Computer Uses: County Counsel of San Diego - Juvenile Dependency Division*

During the same trip to California, I also met with the staff of the County Counsel of San Diego Juvenile Dependency Division (JDD). Their appellate team told me about technology they've set up to make them some of the leading appellate attorneys in the child welfare field in California.

They use several different tools, some new and some older but still functional:

***Brief and Motion Banks:*** One of the things that gets the most use is the Brief and Motion Banks. All briefs and motions filed by the appellate team are entered into a networked computer system that everyone can access. At the top of each brief is the name of the attorney who handled the case, the case outcome, and any comments about the reasoning of the case. The Bank is in Microsoft Word format and organized in four separate subdirectories: appellate briefs and writ responses; motions; briefing in published decisions; and briefing done by the team in California Supreme Court cases. Anyone in the office can use the search function to locate useful briefs or motions. For example, someone could search for phrases, like the subject of the brief, or by case citations. The Brief Bank currently contains 531 briefs.

Although the Brief Bank is used daily by members of the appellate team, attorneys who are not on the appellate team also use it regularly, searching for briefs that address legal issues they will be facing in trial. This can provide them with material for a trial brief or simply help them develop their arguments and authorities to cite to the court. They can also go to the attorney who handled the appeal to get more information about the legal arguments.

According to Kathryn Krug, Senior Deputy County Counsel and attorney in charge of keeping the Brief and Motions Banks up-to-date, this sort of interaction happens all the time. In addition to using the briefs and motions to make better records at the trial court level for future appeals, it really helps the trial attorneys to prepare cases with similar issues. For example, the issue of when the agency can deny a parent reunification services has been briefed many times by the appellate team, since California has 15 grounds for denying reunification services. Not surprisingly, it is also an issue that regularly comes up in court. The trial attorneys use the Brief Bank to get current information when preparing for trial on this issue.

***The Compendium:*** Another computerized tool the appellate attorneys use is the Compendium. This is a large collection – both on computer and in hard copy – of excerpts from appellate briefs, case law updates, practice tips, and canned language on recurring issues, such as grounds for jurisdiction, reasonable efforts, and termination of parental rights, training material, and important inter-office memoranda.

Like the Brief Bank, the Compendium is in Microsoft Word format and the attorneys can use the search function to find the language or case they need. There is a shared directory attached to the Compendium as well. Often the appellate attorneys use it to cut and paste language used in many briefs. The trial attorneys often take the hard copy to court and use it as a trial notebook. The Compendium is also shared with county counsels throughout California at the twice annual Child Welfare Study Section meeting of the California County Counsels' Association.

***REJIS System:*** The Regional Electronic Juvenile Information System (REJIS) is the San Diego court computer system. The JDD, agency, courts, children's attorneys and parents' attorneys developed the system seven years ago after two years of collaboration. REJIS is an internal secure database.

The JDD and the agency are linked to Regis. From their office, JDD and agency staff can get a list of all hearings in the case, and all court orders ("minute orders"), which state the judge's order, the parties attending the hearing, and the date of the next hearing. They can find out where a file is located and the stage of proceedings. Additionally, they can enter court-related information into the system. Other parties, such as the children's

*Finally, Internet e-mail allows them to exchange ideas with other county counsels around the state doing similar work and facing similar issues.[12]*

attorneys and parents' attorneys have access to some of the information on the system. Finally, the JDD uses REJIS as an internal file management system.[10]

***Q & A Computer System:*** The Q & A computer system is an older system in the JDD office, but it is still helpful. This is an internal database that follows three or four different types of cases including appeals and termination cases. This case tracking system is designed to tell the attorney what needs to be done on a particular case, what the timeline for the case is, and the status of the case. The JDD plans to update the system, but it helps the appellate attorneys track cases.

***Child Welfare Study Section Bulletin Board:*** In California, there is a County Counsel Association with a subcommittee for child welfare attorneys. This association sponsors conferences and provides networking opportunities. The JDD was recently connected to the Statewide County Counsel Network and to its Child Welfare Study Section bulletin board — a secure website requiring a password for access. According to Gary Seiser, who heads the JDD appellate team, this will provide another great way to share ideas with other county counsel throughout the state. JDD staff is also considering posting the Compendium on the web site.[11]

***Internet Access:*** All JDD attorneys and paralegals have Internet access from their desktop computers. This enables the appellate team to check the California Judicial Council's website every day for new published appellate decisions or proposed rule changes. It also allows them to track pending legislation or look for legislative history of new changes to dependency statutes through the website for the California Legislature. Finally, Internet e-mail allows them to exchange ideas with other county counsels around the state doing similar work and facing similar issues.[12]

Certainly without very good lawyers, paralegals and support staff, the computerized tools would not be effective. However the JDD has developed systems to improve their practice and work more efficiently. Because of the Brief and Motions Banks and the Compendium, for instance, attorneys do not have to recreate work that has been done before. They can find the information easily and paste it into the brief they are working on. While the appellate team hopes to have faster, better computers, with improved research capabilities some day, they are using their existing resources to their fullest potential.

For more information about the use of technology in the JDD contact Kathryn Krug (kkrugxcc@co.san-diego.ca.us) and Gary Seiser (gseisecc@co.san-diego.ca.us) at 619/ 495-5681.

*Using Bridges, attorneys can access any case from their county, and supervisors can access cases throughout New Hampshire... Bridges allows the agency attorneys to generate forms, reports and statistics.*

### *Computer Networking: New Hampshire Department of Health and Human Services, Division of Children Youth and Families*

The New Hampshire Department of Health and Human Services, Division of Children Youth and Families (DCYF) is on its way to becoming a "paperless office" after installing the Bridges database in 1997. Bridges is a sophisticated database containing case information entered by social workers. Oklahoma received federal grants to develop a computer system with the understanding that it would share the system with other states. New Hampshire DCYF obtained the system and received further federal funds to adapt the system.

Using Bridges, attorneys can access any case from their county, and supervisors can access cases throughout New Hampshire. In addition to being able to review case information, Bridges allows the agency attorneys to generate forms, reports and statistics. When pulled up on a screen, the case information contains nearly everything related to the case including service payment authorization. The only information not included is third party data.

Agency attorneys can also use Bridges to access information about in-office-training sessions. Generally these training sessions are on social work topics that are also helpful to the DCYF attorneys. Ongoing training on Bridges is provided regularly for new staff and attorneys wishing to learn new program features.

When troubles arise with the program, DCYF staff are able to contact a 24-hour hotline for support. During business hours, on-site staff are also available to fix specific hardware and/or software problems. The biggest downside to Bridges is that social workers spend many hours entering data, taking time away from their cases. However, the past two years have proven that the social workers can work on their cases while spending time on the Bridges program.[13]

***Using Common Forms: Franklin County Children's Services – Office of General Counsel, Columbus Ohio***

In Columbus, Ohio, the in-house attorneys represent children's services in termination of parental rights cases. They have developed a set of common forms to efficiently handle their large caseload. The forms are on the computer or can be used in hard copy. Examples of these time-saving forms are:

- ❑ ***Screening form*** — the caseworker fills out a form to identify the grounds for a termination of parental rights. The form requires detail for each ground, such as whether evaluations have been done, evaluation results, the amount of visitation, etc. After submitting the form, an attorney will meet with the caseworker for a staffing on the case to pull information from the file, and prepare an affidavit for filing.
- ❑ ***Checklist*** — at the staffing the attorney will provide the caseworker with a checklist of any information or materials needed to fill in holes from the case file and file the termination petition.
- ❑ ***Termination petition*** — the paralegal has a form to help draft the actual petition.
- ❑ ***Trial preparation form*** — at the staffing, the attorney gives the caseworker a standard form explaining what to expect at the termination hearing. Closer to the trial, the attorney will meet with the caseworker for in-person preparation.

- ❑ ***Case update form*** — after all hearings, the attorney will fill out a form about the case outcome. There are questions about notice and discovery issues. The form is given to the paralegal who peforms follow-up tasks.
- ❑ ***Discovery forms*** — the office has boilerplate letters concerning exchange of discovery. When an attorney is assigned to a case, the general counsel clerical staff automatically sends the letter to inform the attorney about the availability of the file and documentation.
- ❑ ***Indian Child Welfare Act (ICWA) form*** — the office has a standard form, set up as a family tree, to obtain information about the child going back two generations. The office sends the form to the Native American Council in Akron, Ohio for them to contact the tribe if appropriate.

These standard forms save attorneys and paralegals time, add to the office's efficiency, and are another strategy to make the most of available resources.[14]

***Effective Use of the Computer: Department of Health and Human Services, Legal Services Division, Lincoln, Nebraska***

Agency attorneys in Nebraska are spread throughout the state. The central office with four attorneys is in Lincoln. There are also two in Omaha, one in central Nebraska in Kearney, and one in North Platte. Each attorney is assigned a specific area of the state, generally a large geographic region.

With attorneys spread out all over the state, e-mail becomes a useful communication tool. Mike Rumbaugh, legal counsel for the Nebraska Department of Health and Human Services, even went so far to say "e-mail is an amazingly effective tool for us."[15] Nebraska uses two separate internal e-

*Contact other public offices in your community. Find out: What kind of system they use; how much it cost them; and who in the area helped them develop and install it.*

mail systems to communicate with attorneys throughout the state. The attorneys rely on e-mail to communicate about legal strategies and procedures and the legal background of cases. The attorneys are aware of confidentiality issues and, therefore, avoid discussing case specifics via e-mail. They conduct monthly telephone conference calls or team meetings to discuss problems and current status of cases.

All staff, including those in Omaha, Kearney and North Platte, are connected to Westlaw and the Internet. The attorneys have access to a statewide mainframe called STAIRS that contains statutes, cases, and attorney general opinions. They also have access to CWIS (Child Welfare Information System), a detailed database containing social worker case information. This system can help attorneys gather details about individual cases and to "inform policy and set priorities" for Nebraska, such as defining appropriate caseloads.[16]

### Practice Ideas

Some ideas for expanding technology:

- ❑ If you are not very knowledgeable about computers and technology, take an informal survey of your staff. Find the people who could help you brainstorm about your office needs and how to fulfill them. These people may be able to help you find the best systems and applications for your office.

- ❑ Contact other public offices in your community. Find out: What kind of system they use; how much it cost them; and who in the area helped them develop and install it.
- ❑ For information about purchasing legal specific software or locating computer consultants, contact the ABA Legal Technology Resource Center, 312/988-5465.
- ❑ For information about the practical applications of technology, contact the ABA Law Practice Management Section, 312/988-5619. Web site: ***www.abanet.org/LPM***.
- ❑ Contact the Association of Legal Administrators (ALA), 175 East Hawthorn Parkway, Suite 325, Vernon Hills, IL, 60061-1428; 847/816-1212. Web site: www.alanet.org. The ALA provides information on all topics related to managing a law office, including information about computers, case management systems and vendors for these systems.
- ❑ Think broadly. When you learn about a system think about how you could adapt it for your office. Learn about the court and agency's computer systems and decide whether your office should be linked to it.
- ❑ Contact local companies who conduct computer trainings. They may be able to customize training sessions to fit your needs.
- ❑ Look into purchasing your state statutes on CD-ROM. This may save you money and library space.

## CONCLUSION

This chapter describes some creative ways agency attorney offices are using available resources to help their staffs work efficiently and as "hassle free" as possible. It's likely you have other innovative ideas not described here. Almost everyone in the child welfare field desires more resources. However much can be done by using available resources creatively. You probably can't change everything at once, but develop a long-range plan for improvements and step-by-step you can make the reforms you hope for. Take action.

## ENDNOTES

1. Snyder, Theda C. *Running a Law Practice on a Shoestring*. Chicago: American Bar Association, 1997, 94, 102.

2. Telephone interview with Sherri Kaplan, legal assistant supervisor, Philadelphia Law Department Health and Human Services Unit, March 30, 1999.

3. Snyder at 123.

4. *Guide for Legal Assistant Education Programs*. Chicago: American Bar Association Standing Committee on Legal Assistants, 1998.

5. Interview with Valencia Saffold, Administrative Support Officer, County Counsel of Santa Clara County – Child Dependency Unit, March 10, 1999.

6. Ibid.

7. Group interview during attorney meeting, County Counsel of Santa Clara County – Child Dependency Unit, March 9, 1999.

8. Snyder at 118-120; Interview with Diane Bennett and Mike Clark, Lead Deputy County Counsel, County Counsel of Santa Clara County – Child Dependency Unit, March 8, 1999.

9. Telephone interview with Mike Rumbaugh, Department of Health and Human Services, Legal Services Division Legal Counsel, Lincoln, Nebraska, April 14, 1999.

10. Telephone interview with Susan Strom, Chief Deputy County Counsel, San Diego, CA, April 20, 1999.

11. Group interview with appellate team, County Counsel of San Diego County – Juvenile Dependency Division, March 11, 1999; Telephone interview with Kathryn Krug, Senior Deputy County Counsel, Certified Legal Specialist in Family Law, County Counsel of San Diego, CA, March 30, 1999; Telephone interview with Gary Seiser, Senior Deputy County Counsel, Team Leader and Appellate Team, County Counsel of San Diego, CA, April 20, 1999.

12. Interview with Gary Seiser.

13. Telephone interview with James Anderson, DCYF Staff Attorney, Concord, New Hampshire, April 15, 1999.

14. Telephone interview with Melissa Mitchell, General Counsel, Franklin County Children Services, Columbus, Ohio, April 15, 1999.

15. Telephone interview with Mike Rumbaugh.

16. Ibid.

CHAPTER 8:

# Agency Attorneys and Casewokers: Working Well Together

## HOW OFTEN HAVE YOU HEARD:

**Agency Attorney:**

- ❑ "Those social workers are so 'touchy/ feely' they can't give the judge concrete facts."
- ❑ "The workers are always 'in the field,' where is that!?"

**Child Welfare Agency Caseworker:**

- ❑ "Our agency attorneys are so arrogant and emotionally distant..."
- ❑ "The attorneys care more about winning the case than about the kids."

**Attorney and Caseworker:**

- ❑ "They never return my call."
- ❑ "They just don't understand what I do..."

As an agency attorney representing the Department of Human Services in Philadelphia, I often heard these kinds of comments. At times I felt like a cruise director — trying to keep caseworkers and attorneys happy by coordinating their activities and helping them work together better. Sometimes, "cheerleading" about working as a team would improve life, but usually just for a little while. What we needed was some real effort and communication to improve our relationships.

If you also hear these gripes in the halls of your office, read on for a "beyond cheerleading" discussion of ways to ease the tensions in attorney/caseworker relationships and to form positive working teams. There's more to it than saying, "Let's all be friends..."

## ROLES OF ATTORNEYS AND SOCIAL WORKERS

### Defining the Client

As an agency attorney, it is important that you define your client. Many conflicts between attorneys and social workers stem from a misunderstanding of who the attorney represents.

The models of agency representation vary by jurisdiction and should be defined by your state's law. Attorneys may be employed by local prosecutor's offices, state attorney general offices, local civil litigation offices, or the agency itself. Additionally, some agencies hire special prosecutors or contract attorneys.[1] If you are uncertain what your state legislation dictates, your state attorney general office should be able to advise.

Within each model, the view of who the client is differs. Some represent the agency as an entity, relying on the caseworker's opinions, but keeping the interests of the agency in mind at all times, and some, as in the prosecutor model, represent the "people." Each has its strengths and weaknesses.

If you represent the agency as an entity, as I did in my previous practice, there are two considerations. Sometimes the caseworkers feel the attorneys disregard their wishes, and do not represent them aggressively in court. What happens is the agency

*Sometimes the interests of the agency differ from those of individual caseworkers.*

attorneys try to be mindful of agency policy, while listening to the individual caseworker's viewpoint. Sometimes the interests of the agency differ from those of individual caseworkers. Because the attorney represents the agency, not individual caseworkers, the attorney must defer to the agency.

The other concern is that if caseworkers make serious errors that conflict with agency policy and a contempt proceeding is held, the caseworkers' union attorney has to represent the caseworker, while the agency attorney represents the agency. In my experience, the benefits of this model outweighed the problems. We were able to consistently represent agency policy while advocating for the caseworkers' positions in court.

Several concerns about the prosecutor model make this method of representation particularly problematic. Often, the attorneys in these offices are new and choose to work in the prosecutor's office to practice criminal law. They rotate out of dependency cases quickly, and therefore never get proper training. As a result, the caseworkers often feel the representation is not adequate. Additionally, with this method the attorneys generally get the final word on whether a petition should be filed. This leaves the caseworker feeling as if his or her professional opinion is not considered. Caseworkers may also fear that with attorneys making decisions about the caseworkers' clients, best social work practice will be ignored.

*Often, attorneys worry that if the caseworkers are making major decisions about a case, the attorneys will be forced to do something unethical.*

The National Association of Social Workers (NASW) *Standards for Social Work Practice* in child protection set out: "The initiation of court action is an agency team decision requiring legal counsel and legal representation." In the prosecutor model of representation, the collaborative decision-making process can get lost and can cause tension between you and the caseworker.

No matter which model your jurisdiction uses, it is important for you to define your client.[3] Further, it is important for your client to understand the scope of your representation.

### Remember Your Obligations

No matter who your client is, there are certain ethical obligations you have in your practice. You may need to communicate these rules to the caseworker from time to time. Your primary responsibility is as follows: "A lawyer shall provide competent representation to a client. Competent representation requires the legal knowledge, skill, thoroughness and preparation reasonably necessary for the representation."[4] Further, "In representing a client, a lawyer shall exercise independent professional judgment and render candid advice. In rendering advice, a lawyer may refer not only to law, but to other considerations such as moral, economic, social and political factors, that may be relevant to the client's situation."[5]

As an agency attorney, you will often be asked to act as an advisor. You must provide the best counsel possible and then allow your client to reach a decision.

Often, attorneys worry that if the caseworkers are making decisions about a case, the attorneys will be forced to do something unethical. If you and the caseworker or supervisor disagree about a decision, you have an obligation to try to work out a solution that is comfortable for you and the client. You are bound by the Model Rules of Professional Conduct, however, and may not act in an unethical manner. Generally, if you and your client discuss the matter, you will be able to reach a mutually acceptable outcome.

### Define Responsibilities

Decide which tasks you should handle and which should be handled by the caseworker. Decide what jobs should be shared. Deciding who has what responsibilities and sticking with it often causes tension in the attorney/caseworker relationship. Deciding together can make your team operate more smoothly.

Use the table on p. 8–116 when deciding who should handle various duties. Your needs may be different and you may have additional tasks that should be considered when you and the caseworkers divide the workload.

You and the caseworkers should make your own list of jobs and openly discuss who should have primary responsibility for each. Consider creating protocols for some of the ongoing responsibilities you share. With the written protocol for termination petitions, for example, both you, your staff and the caseworker will have guidance about what jobs you

| Responsibility | Who Should Do It |
|---|---|
| Investigate report | Caseworker |
| Discuss facts with police, medical professionals, teachers | Caseworker — may have discussions with attorney |
| Prepare petition | Legal assistant with information from caseworker and supervision of attorney |
| Notify parties of hearing | Law office by subpoena — if required; caseworker |
| Identify witnesses | Attorney — may have help from legal assistant |
| Prepare witnesses | Attorney — may have help from legal assistant |
| Prepare child witness | Attorney — may have caseworker present to emotionally support child; don't forget to collaborate with child's attorney or CASA |
| Prepare exhibits for hearing | Legal assistant and attorney;caseworker should provide organized case file |
| Other court preparation | Attorney with conversations with caseworker |
| Present case in court | Attorney |
| Enter into agreements with parents | Parents' attorney should be present; caseworker and/or attorney can work with parents and other should be included before agreement finalized |
| Ongoing documentation | Caseworker |
| Attend meetings with family | Caseworker and sometimes attorney |
| Ongoing casework | Caseworker |
| Decide when to terminate parental rights | Caseworker in consultation with attorney; judge |
| Refer case from criminal prosecution | Caseworker |

must each complete and timeframes for completion. See page 8-126 for sample protocol concerning termination of parental rights petitions.

### Decide Who Calls the Shots

Once you have defined your responsibilities, you and the workers need to decide who makes the decisions. Some will be fairly obvious. For example, if an issue clearly involves a legal strategy, you get to make the final decision.[6] Similarly, if the question concerns social work or family specific treatment, the worker, on behalf of the agency, calls the shots.

Most questions though, are not so clearly defined. Your strong communication and teamwork will be needed to discuss the issue with the caseworker and try to resolve the issue in a manner that satisfies both of your goals.

Additionally, you will need to keep in mind the answer to the "who is my client?" question. Generally, your client will be the agency and not the worker. You and the agency administration should have a system in place to resolve conflicts between you and individual workers. Sometimes just having a calm conversation with the worker and both of your supervisors can help. Sometimes the issue has systemic impact and the head of the agency needs to make the decision. If a dispute resolution system is implemented before a major conflict, none of the players will be offended if the system is used.[7] There are times when you will need to talk with the caseworker's supervisor for clarification. This should not be viewed as "tattling" on the caseworker, but part of the process to improve and expand the team. See box on next page for sample protocol.

## Sample Protocol for Dispute Resolution Between Agency Attorney & Caseworker

*Step 1.* You and the caseworker thoroughly and calmly discuss the case or problem.

*Step 2.* If you cannot resolve the problem, each of you go and discuss it with your supervisors. Pick a time to communicate again within two days.

*Step 3.* Meet with your supervisors and determine whether you are taking the position of your agency. Try to work out other ways to view the issue. Find out when your supervisor is free to meet with the caseworker and supervisor if needed. This should be within one week, or sooner if the case is pending in court.

*Step 4.* Keep the appointment to talk again and see if there has been a resolution.

*Step 5.* If there was no resolution, pick a mutually convenient time for a meeting between you and the caseworker and your supervisors.

*Step 6.* Have the meeting. Try to talk through the entire issue to reach an understanding.

*Step 7.* If there is still no resolution, you will each need to go up your chain of command. If this is a policy issue, the head of your unit will need to discuss it with the head of the agency and find a reasonable position.

## NEED FOR COLLABORATION

As an agency attorney, you need good relationships with child welfare agency caseworkers to best serve children in the system. When you and the workers are busy complaining, your ability to work as a team and handle cases effectively and efficiently suffers. As a result, your cases may not be prepared thoroughly for court, your frustration about your job may increase and the children on your caseload may remain in foster care longer than they should.

There are several characteristics of a strong working relationship:

### Communicate

Open communication is a basic element of any good relationship. It is no different when working with caseworkers. Communicating effectively requires returning phone calls promptly, asking questions, addressing differences of opinion, and making time to talk about cases. Caseworkers should expect this of you and you of them.

Work with the caseworkers to devise a workable communication system. Do you all have e mail and are you using it? Is this a way to communicate that would save time and be reliable? Do you have an inter-office mail system? Are there mutually agreed upon times that you could be available to answer questions? Explore what, if any, complaints you each have about availability and level of communication and then, together, find ways to improve. When you are all communicating there is less likelihood that you will arrive in court not knowing what the caseworker's position is or what needs to be done for the child.

### Develop Mutual Respect

Attorneys and caseworkers are both professionals with specific areas of expertise. You both have particular tasks to perform on all cases and are essential to a positive outcome in the case. Often, attorneys and caseworkers express that members of the other profession do not value their opinions and do not treat them courteously. When there is a lack of respect, incorrect assumptions about the other group emerge and add to negative feelings. It is essential that you each learn about the other's backgrounds and job responsibilities. With greater understanding of each other an increased respect will grow.

### Build Trust

In addition to respect, you and the caseworkers need to trust each other. If you are a new attorney it can be difficult to gain the trust of the caseworkers. The caseworkers may believe you do not know the answers to questions or are too new to advocate aggressively on their behalf. If you consistently provide good advice and perform well in court, the caseworkers will develop trust.

If you are an experienced attorney and have gained the caseworker's trust, keeping it requires that you are consistent and honest. When a trusting relationship exists, the caseworkers are more likely to call you with questions rather than acting first and then asking. Similarly, when you trust the workers, you will have greater confidence in the cases you present in court.

### Teamwork

Out of the communication, respect and trust comes a sense of teamwork.[8] When you and the caseworker know what the other has been doing on a case, know what the other person thinks about the case and value the other person's viewpoint, the case will be its strongest and the child will benefit. Even if you and the caseworker do not agree about parts of the case, as a team you will be able to reach a mutually satisfactory decision. If you are functioning as a team, your representation will be its best and the caseworker's efforts for the family will be most effective.

### Strengthening the Relationship

To improve the attorney/caseworker relationship you need to talk and have more contact with each other. You and the caseworkers are probably overloaded in managing your day-to-day work, and the idea of trainings or group discussions may not be a pleasant one. However, taking time now will help improve the team for the long-term.

### Informal Sessions

***Find Shared Beliefs.*** Meet with caseworkers and agency administrators to eliminate existing barriers and identify common goals. You will probably all realize that you share the ideal of improving the lives of children in your community and working through your differences may become easier with this understanding.

The *NASW Standards for Social Work Practice in Child Protection* delineate specific values that are central to improving the child welfare system and the lives of children and families. These include: recognizing the dignity of the child; making a commitment to the child's family; promoting permanent and consistent care for children; and recognizing people's capacity to change.[9]

Child welfare attorneys generally share these ideals and the caseworkers need to know that.

**Facilitate in Comfort.**

Ask a neutral person with experience controlling discussions to facilitate a series of sessions that allow participants to express concerns and work towards concrete remedies. If you do not have a person in your department with this kind of experience, consider contacting your local university's marketing department for referrals. Meet in a comfortable room. You and the caseworkers can alternate as hosts if your offices are not in the same place.

***Be Concrete.*** It may start as gripe and complaint sessions, and sometimes it is necessary for people to express their frustrations before being able to form positive resolutions. If complaining is permitted, the facilitator should set ground rules. For instance, names should not be used to bad mouth one another.

As an example of the need to be concrete, I remember an experience several years ago in Philadelphia. The caseworkers and attorneys in my office attempted to have some sessions focused on improving our relationships. The attorneys often found them frustrating because there was too much talking with too few concrete results. While we cared how the caseworkers felt about us and the court process, we were more interested in trying to "fix" the problems right away. Needless to say, we were unable to do so without also talking about our view of the system and really listening to what the caseworkers were sharing. Similarly, the process

*There needs to be an understanding that, in general, attorneys and social workers think about things differently.*

## Top 10 Benefits of Teamwork

1. Better and more timely results for children and families
2. Cases move more smoothly
3. Everyone feels included
4. Decisions reached by consensus
5. Work done more efficiently
6. Lower likelihood of burnout
7. A better understanding of the whole system and how it operates
8. Opportunity to learn about a whole new profession/expand your horizons
9. Understand each other's language
10. Improved morale

## Top 10 Things We Need From Each Other

*Source: Based on interviews with Melissa Mitchell, J.D., General Counsel, Franklin County Children Services, Columbus, Ohio; Anne Marie Lancour, J.D., Legal Training Director, ABA Center on Children and the Law, Washington, D.C.; and Heidi Redlich, MSW, J.D., State Training Director, ABA Center on Children and the Law, Washington, D.C., July 14, 1998.*

could not work without the caseworkers joining us in trying to think of practical ways to improve our relationships.

***Understand Each Others' Languages.*** There needs to be an understanding that, in general, attorneys and social workers think about things differently. They do not always use the same language. Attorneys are taught and are generally good at "multi-tasking," while caseworkers concentrate on single tasks, such as working on specific goals with a family. Attorneys often look at things on a macro or system level, whereas caseworkers focus on the child or family level. Attorneys have good intuitive adversarial skills while caseworkers have intuitive social skills. These social skills are necessary for good social work, but may not be useful when it comes to testifying in a courtroom where the adversarial skills come in handy.

Additionally, attorneys are not trained in social work practice while in law school and caseworkers learn very little about the law during their educations. The law is pervasive in the child welfare system which may be frustrating for caseworkers who focus on helping families.[1] To improve the relationships, attorneys and caseworkers must acknowledge these differences and try to learn each others' languages.

***Share Basic Information.*** Often attorneys and caseworkers complain that the other group does not understand what they do or their roles. During discussion sessions you could talk about how you came to your positions and what your jobs entail. A caseworker could describe a home visit and the feelings that accompany removing a child from the home. You could discuss how you prepare for a contested hearing and the difficulties involved in getting attached to one of the children. Let the workers know that "lawyers have feelings too!"

***Reach Outcomes.*** You are busy and so are the caseworkers, but try not to let the discussions end until you have realized some positive outcomes. Try to develop some protocols like the ones on the next page. Other areas in which protocols could help are:

- ❑ When attorneys should attend meetings between the caseworker and a family.
- ❑ The expected responsibilities of the attorneys and workers in preparing a solid case for court.
- ❑ Implementing an information system to inform everyone about changes in staff, law and policy.
- ❑ How workers and attorneys will communicate: e-mail, written memos, telephone conferencing.
- ❑ What the dispute resolution system is and when it will be used.

If not all attorneys and caseworkers attend the sessions, develop a way to share the protocols and the other new approaches with the rest of the staff.

### Interdisciplinary Training

In addition to informal sessions, it is helpful for you and the caseworkers to attend substantive trainings in areas that relate to both of your practices.

By participating in the trainings together, you will all have the same knowledge base. You will also

*To improve the relationships, attorneys and caseworkers must acknowledge these differences and try to learn each others' languages.*

## Sample Protocol for Termination Petitions

*Step 1.* A recommendation is made by the permanency planning committee, legal unit, or supervisor that a termination petition be filed.

*Step 2.* Within **30 days** of Step 1, the caseworker will send a completed information packet with referral form to the legal unit.

*Step 3.* For a permanent neglect, mental illness or mental retardation case, within **30 days** of Step 2, the attorney will either draft a petition or request more information from the caseworker. The attorney will forward the draft petition or request for information to the caseworker.

For an abandonment case, within **15 days** of Step 2, the attorney will either draft a petition or request more information from the caseworker. The attorney will forward the draft petition or request for information to the caseworker.

*Step 4.* If additional information is requested, the caseworker shall return the petition or provide the information to the attorneys within **7 days**. Once the petition is returned, the attorney shall file the petition within **7 days**.

*Step 5.* After receiving the additional information, for a permanent neglect, mental illness or mental retardation case, the attorneys shall file the petition within **30 days**.

After receiving the additional information, for an abandonment case, the attorney shall file the petition within **15 days**.

*Step 6.* The attorney and caseworker shall meet at least **2 weeks** prior to the trial date to prepare for trial.

*Source: Albany County Permanency Planning Project, Attorney Caseworker Protocol for Termination Petitions. Developed by Anne Marie Lancour, J.D., Legal Training Director, ABA Center on Children and the Law. Washington, D.C.*

benefit from spending time together outside the courtroom. While interdisciplinary training cannot resolve all issues between you and the caseworkers and it will not provide you with all of the strictly legal knowledge that you need, it is an excellent way for everyone to develop their skills and knowledge.

Topics to consider for training include:

- ❑ Invite a local judge to discuss court practice, the type of testimony he or she prefers, what should be included in a petition, and his or her view of how the court process relates to the child welfare system as a whole.
- ❑ Invite a local doctor/medical expert to talk about the medical evidence that points to abuse, Munchausen Syndrome by Proxy, failure to thrive and other medical issues that relate to child welfare. The discussion can also focus on the ethical decisions involved when a parent withholds medical treatment for religious reasons.
- ❑ Have a psychiatrist or psychologist discuss mental health diagnoses and the implications for parents and foster children who suffer from the disorders.
- ❑ Learn about the substance abuse programs available in your community and how they can be accessed for the children and their parents.

### Multidisciplinary Teams

In Washington, the agency attorneys and caseworkers have improved their relationships and their effectiveness in cases through two types of multidisciplinary meetings. First, for children, especially young children under three years, who have been in foster care for three months, the agency has a prognostic staffing meeting. An attorney attends, and the team reviews the case to determine whether a concurrent plan should be implemented.

The caseworkers appreciate having the attorney attend and have found these meetings help reduce the time the child remains in foster care. Because the attorney knows the state legislation, he or she can advise whether the case is ready for a termination of parental rights petition or another permanent plan. Additionally, the attorneys and caseworkers get to know each other better which improves their teamwork in all cases.

Additionally, the courts in Washington have initiated committees made up of judges, agency attorneys, caseworkers or supervisors and defense attorneys to resolve procedural problems in the court. Through these committees, the court has reduced delays in cases, the participants have gained respect for each other, the judges have taken a positive leadership role, and all players work together to resolve the problems that affect the entire system.[12]

## CONCLUSION

No matter what kind of relationship you have with the caseworkers in your agency, there is probably room for improvement. While it is not easy and may be frustrating, through increased communication and a focus on mutual respect you can work as a more effective team to benefit the children and families in your community.

## ENDNOTES


1 . Duquette, Donald N. "Lawyers' Roles in Child Protection." In *The Battered Child*, 5th ed., by Mary Edna Helfer, Ruth S.Kempe and Richard D. Krugman. Chicago and London: The University of Chicago Press, 1997. Plum, Henry J. *Legal Representation of Agencies Presentation Outline*. June 15-17, 1998.

2. *NASW Standards for Social Work Practice in Child Protection.* Standard 21. Washington, D.C.: NASW, 1997.

3. See Rule 1.13 and commentary. *Model Rules of Professional Conduct*. Chicago: American Bar Association, 1997. ("A lawyer employed or retained by an organization [including a governmental organization] represents the organization acting through its duly authorized constituents")

4. Ibid. at Rule 1.1.

5. Ibid. at Rule 2.1.

6. *See* Rule 1.2 and commentary. *Model Rules of Professional Conduct.*

7. Duquette at 471-72. *See also* Skarin, Gene D. "The Role of the Child Protective Agnecy's Attorney in Family Court." *Practicing Law Institute Criminal Law and Urban Problems* 171, March 1995, 440-41.

8. *See* Weinstein, Janet. "And Never the Twain Shall Meet: The Best Interests of Children and the Adversary System." University of Miami Law Review 52, October 1997, 159.

9. *NASW Standards for Social Work Practice in Child Protection.* Standard 2 and commentary.

10. Telephone interview with Melissa Mitcholl, J.D., General Counsel, Franklin County Children Services, Columbus, Ohio based on her discussions with the in-house attorneys at Franklin County Children Services, July 14, 1998.

11. Herring, David J. "Interdisciplinary Training and Assessing Community Services Resources." In *Agency Attorney Training Manual: Achieving Timely Permanency for Children by Implementing the Private Model of Legal Representation for the State Agency in Child Abuse and Neglect Matters.* Pittsburgh: University of Pittsburgh Law School, 1992. See also Laver, Mimi. "A Guide to Retaining Agency Attorneys." Child Law Practice 17, No. 5, July 1998, 73-75.

12. Telephone interview with Linda Katz, MSW, adjunct faculty at the University of Washington School of Social Work, Seattle, Washington, July 14, 1998.

CHAPTER 9:

# Team Spirit:

## SANTA CLARA COUNTY COUNSEL OFFICE CHILD DEPENDENCY UNIT

To best represent the Santa Clara County Social Services Agency, Department of Family and Children's Services (DFCS), Mike Clark and Diane Bennett, the lead attorneys in the Child Dependency Unit (CDU), have created well organized, close knit teams within the county counsel office and with DFCS. As a result, the attorneys and staff feel supported and the relationship with the agency is continually improving. This emphasis on teamwork translates into open communication with DFCS staff, substantive training for attorneys and caseworkers and judges who boast about the job the county counsel is doing in the court community.[1]

There are a number of elements to the team approach that make the office work well:

### LEAD ATTORNEYS SET THE TONE

Diane and Mike run the office as a team. They know their strengths and have split management duties accordingly. Diane spends more time at the DFCS office and Mike focuses on keeping the unit up-to-date on legislative and case law changes. They both practiced in the unit before becoming lead attorneys and they both still appear in court regularly. Perhaps most importantly, they both have an open door policy for the entire staff despite their very busy schedules at court, meetings, DCFS office hours, and teaching. As one of the attorneys said,

"Mike and Diane are great leads. They are supportive and do a good job of taking care of things with the client and main office so the attorneys are free to do their jobs."[2]

### Regular Meetings and Trainings for the CDU

While some attorneys told me that they would like to attend more out-of-the-office trainings, and Mike "wished" for a more formalized mentoring program, unit attorneys and staff regularly meet and share information. These meetings include:

***Monthly lead meeting*** — Diane, Mike, Jennifer Allmand, the lead court assistant/ paralegal, and Valencia Saffold, the Administrative Support Officer discuss issues facing the office as a whole.

***Monthly floor meeting*** — the entire staff shares information, celebrates birthdays and discusses office issues.

***Lunch meetings*** — the attorneys meet three or four times a month to share information, deal with frustrations, and receive training in clinical and practice issues. I attended one of these meetings — while it was fun and there was a clear sense of camaraderie — it was also clear the attorneys valued it as "learning time."

***Second Chair Program*** — this is part of new attorney training. The new attorney first observes in court, and then second chairs a trial with a more experienced attorney. The more experienced attorney then second chairs another trial with the new attorney. This provides the new attorney with support and confidence as he or she starts a career as a trial lawyer.

***County Counsel Association Conferences*** — each attorney in the office gets to attend one of two statewide county counsel meetings a year. These meetings provide training in relevant legal issues as well as an opportunity to meet with California attorneys who do similar work.

### Career Track Status

Attorneys come to the CDU with a great deal of prior experience in child welfare and courtroom practice. The attorneys and management view their jobs as career track; generally they are not rotated in or out. They are paid relatively well compared with other government attorneys and are provided with up to date technological support.

### Office Hours at DCFS

Two mornings a week, Diane Bennett has office hours at the DCFS office. Caseworkers and other staff can stop by and ask Diane legal questions about their cases. The caseworkers are always free to telephone the attorneys with other questions, but the office hours provide an opportunity to really analyze an issue with an attorney. It also is a time for the caseworkers to get to know the legal staff and forge a good, working relationship.

### Monthly Brown Bag Lunch Series

On the fourth Thursday of each month, one or more attorneys from the CDU spend the lunch hour with caseworkers discussing legal issues. Caseworker participation is voluntary and there are about 25 workers at each session. Topics have included:

- legislative changes

*The attorneys and management view their jobs as career track; generally they are not rotated in or out.*

*...participants discussed the roles of attorneys and DCFS, developing strategies for managing case crises as an effective team.*

- ❑ reasonable services for incarcerated clients
- ❑ Indian Child Welfare Act
- ❑ how to read a rap sheet
- ❑ when to consider a reunification bypass (proceeding to seek a new permanent placement for the child without first providing reunification services)
- ❑ paternity issues

This program educates the caseworkers on important legal topics, gives the attorneys opportunities to teach and interact with their client, and everyone gets to know each other better.

### Forensic Human Services — A Certificate Program for Human Service Professionals

The Forensic Human Services program has been in existence for six years. It consists of 150 classroom hours set up in six different courses. The classes are scheduled after work and participation is voluntary. Several CDU attorneys are on the faculty of the program and County Counsel is one of six sponsors, along with DCFS, the Superior Court and San Jose State University's Graduate School of Social Work. I observed one class in which Penny Blake, the supervising attorney at the District Attorney's office told the group what the child's attorney looks for in a good court report. See Appendix xxx for the full curriculum of the program.

### Managers, Supervisors, and County Counsel Offsite

On President's Day, 1999, the Santa Clara Superior Court was closed. DCFS and the CDU took the opportunity to hold a joint meeting of the CDU attorneys and DCFS management staff. During this program, participants discussed the roles of attorneys and DCFS, developing strategies for managing case crises as an effective team. Participants also talked about legal and service trends in child welfare. The program was the first of its kind. It was another out-of-court way attorneys and DCFS develop their relationship and improve their services to children and youth in Santa Clara County.

## CONCLUSION

This chapter highlights how the CDU effectively represents DCFS. Supporting one another and working as a team are key to CDU effectiveness. As a team, the CDU can laugh, learn, and provide excellent representation to its client. By expanding the team to include DCFS, the attorneys are best able to protect the children in the community.[3]

## ENDNOTES

1. Interview with the Honorable Leonard Edwards, San Jose, CA, March 9, 1999.

2. Interview with Karen Heggie, Deputy County Counsel, Santa Clara County Office of the County Counsel, Child Dependency Unit, March 9, 1999.

3. This chapter was based on interviews and observations of the attorneys and staff of the Santa Clara County Office of the County Counsel, Child Dependency Unit, March 8-10, 1999.

CHAPTER 10:

# Implementing ASFA: A Challenge for Agency Attorneys

When new laws are passed, we in the child welfare system often find ourselves scrambling to figure out what the law is about and more importantly, how it affects our practice. Between court schedules, writing briefs and generally keeping our heads above water, there is not much time left for analyzing complicated statutes. Even if we do get to look at the new law, incorporating it into our daily routine is difficult.

Implementing the federal *Adoption and Safe Families Act* of 1997 (ASFA), P.L. 105-89, is important because it could make a positive difference for many children, but because of the effort, thought and time to make it work effectively, it poses a true challenge.

## ASFA — WHAT YOU SHOULD KNOW

### Health and Safety

With bipartisan support, ASFA was passed by Congress and signed into law by President Clinton in late 1997. The guiding principle of ASFA is that the "child's health and safety shall be the paramount concern."[1] Congress believed many children were not safe in their homes while child welfare agencies were making reasonable efforts to preserve the family. Similarly, there was concern that children were leaving foster care and returning to their biological families without appropriate safety measures in place.[2] Because of the health and safety mandate, children may not stay in inappropriate homes.

**Permanence**

Another theme in ASFA is that children deserve nurturing and permanent homes. Congress included a number of provisions to decrease the time children spend in foster care and increase their chances of achieving permanence.

In most cases, for example, child welfare agencies must continue to make the types of reasonable efforts to preserve and reunify families that they did prior to ASFA. However, under ASFA there are some circumstances under which reasonable efforts to reunify the family will not need to be made. Congress mandated that reasonable efforts not be made when:

- ❑ the case involves certain crimes committed by the parents, such as murder of another child and
- ❑ parental rights to another child were terminated involuntarily

Congress gave states latitude to define additional circumstances, but suggested that states consider including the following types of maltreatment:

- ❑ torture
- ❑ abandonment
- ❑ chronic abuse and
- ❑ sexual abuse[3]

In these cases, a judge must determine that reasonable efforts to reunify the family should not be made. If a judge makes this decision, the judge must conduct a permanency hearing in 30 days. During this hearing, the parties must decide what steps they

*The compelling reasons for not filing a petition may include, for example: the child does not want to be adopted, or the family is making serious progress towards safe reunification.*

will take to ensure permanency for the child and set a timeline to complete the process.[4]

### Timeframes

In cases in which the child welfare agency does work with the family towards reunification, ASFA also sets strict timeframes. If a child remains in foster care for 12 months, the court must hold a permanency hearing to determine an appropriate plan for the child. The hearing must be thorough and specific so all parties leave knowing what the plan for the child is and how they will implement it.[5]

If the child has been in foster care during 15 of the last 22 months, or if at the permanency hearing it appears that reunification is unrealistic, the court may direct the agency to file a termination of parental rights petition. This requirement will be waived only if:

- the child is being cared for by a relative
- if the agency has documented a compelling reason why terminating parental rights would not be in the child's best interests or
- if the agency did not provide the family with necessary reunification services[6]

The compelling reasons for not filing a petition may include, for example: the child does not want to be adopted, or the family is making serious progress towards safe reunification.

When making reasonable efforts to preserve and reunify the family is inconsistent with the child's permanent plan, the agency must then take steps to place the child quickly and finalize the permanency plan.[7]

### Agency Attorney as Point Person

As the agency attorney, you play a pivotal role in bringing about the changes that ASFA demands. You are generally the moving party in cases and it is often your responsibility to file termination of parental rights petitions. You set the pace of the proceedings. Therefore, you must be familiar with ASFA and your state legislation, file petitions in a timely manner, and be prepared for all hearings to move cases efficiently.

***Know the Law*** — The first step in implementing ASFA is knowing what it says. To start, focus your attention on the sections that will most closely affect your practice such as the reasonable efforts, termination of parental rights and permanency hearing requirements. Each state must ensure its legislation complies with ASFA. Some states have already passed new laws and others are currently drafting bills. Get a copy of your state's legislation and compare it with ASFA. You will need to know, for instance, when reasonable efforts to reunify the family are not required or if there are new termination grounds that mirror the reasons to excuse reunification efforts.

---

*While correcting a judge may be uncomfortable, there are ways to tactfully point out ASFA requirements about the individual case.*

---

## 10 Prerequisites for Effective Judicial Implementation of ASFA

1. Child protection agencies have adequate legal representation to make it possible to achieve legally permanent homes for foster children within the timetables specified by ASFA.

2. Courts make changes in judicial infrastructure necessary to make timely decisions.

3. States adopt thorough and carefully thought out provisions to implement the ASFA revisions in reasonable efforts requirements.

4. Permanency hearings cause states to make timely decisions for children in foster care.

5. Agencies quickly gather sufficient information to seek early termination of parental rights when appropriate.

6. At the beginning of each case, agencies and their attorneys formally notify (i.e., serve with summons and petition) noncustodial parents, possible unwed fathers, and relatives.

7. The agency develops thoughtful exceptions to the ASFA requirement to file petitions for termination of parental rights within 15 months. It requires that

caseworkers provide individualized information showing why the exception applies.

8. The child welfare agency provides timely services to preserve families and thus facilitates timely decisions to either return children home or permanently place them with new families.

9. Agencies other than the public child protection agency (e.g. substance abuse treatment and mental health treatment) provide timely services to preserve families and thus facilitate timely decisions to either return children home or permanently place them with new families. Services by other agencies are provided without long waiting lists and the duration of the services are limited to adapt to child welfare agencies' permanency planning deadlines.

10. Child protection agencies obtain enough well-trained staff to recruit adoptive homes and place children in such homes.

*Source: Mark Hardin, Director, Child Welfare, ABA Center on Children and the Law*

***Use What You Have Learned*** — As the person with the ASFA knowledge, you may be called upon to educate others about ASFA's requirements. While it is not your sole responsibility, by spreading the word you may be able to make the court process run more smoothly. Consider organizing a training session for the attorneys and judges in your community. Approach your judges for their input and consider them as possible trainers.

As the child advocates, guardians, parents' attorneys and other players learn the law, you will all have an easier time. With an understanding of ASFA, strategizing with caseworkers and other parties about ways to move particular cases through the system becomes easier. Even if you are unable to organize mass trainings, you may be in a position to educate judges and others on a case-by-case basis. While correcting a judge may be uncomfortable, there are ways to tactfully point out ASFA requirements about the individual case. In addition to saying something at the bar of the court, you could offer to prepare a memorandum of law on the issue. Although a time consuming choice, it may serve to resolve conflict for many other cases in the future.

### Agency Attorney as Counselor

For ASFA to work, the agency must be up to speed on the changes in the law and their practical implications. You can help them get there. There are several areas in which the agency will need your input:

***Document, Document, Document*** — Having a well documented case file is always important, however under ASFA it is essential. To excuse reasonable efforts to reunify the family, you will need to show the court that aggravated circumstances exist making reunification extremely unlikely, or that the parents committed one of a number of crimes or had their rights to another child involuntarily terminated. To meet this burden, agency staff will need to gather evidence such as substance abuse treatment records, hospital records or notes concerning observations of the parent and child.

Throughout the court process, you should present documentation of the parents' progress towards reunification to the judge to help determine the appropriate permanent plan. The caseworker should be able to provide documentation about the parents' compliance with case plan objectives, such as the quality and quantity of visitation and attendance and progress in substance abuse treatment, counseling or parenting classes.

If you are filing a termination of parental rights petition, you will again need similar documentation about the family. If you and the caseworker decide that a termination of parental rights petition should not be filed because it is not in the child's best interests, ASFA requires that compelling reasons for that decision be documented.

Meet with the agency administration to explain these court-related concerns. Together, devise a system for the caseworkers to document their case files consistent with your needs for proving a case and their needs for providing proper casework. Be available to meet with caseworkers and supervisors to help them understand the need for change and the methods to follow.

***Criminal Records*** — Records of criminal convictions are available to the public. You should contact your local criminal records department to determine what procedure they use to release sealed copies of the conviction record. They may require specific information about the person such as birth date, date of conviction or crime, or social security number. They may also require that someone personally comes to retrieve the record.

When you know the procedure, write a simple protocol to distribute through the agency so caseworkers can obtain the information. Similarly, the individual may have a federal conviction or a FBI record. Contact the local branch of the FBI or federal court to see if you can jointly develop a process for getting records.

***Mental Health/Substance Abuse Treatment Records*** — In many cases, you will also want access to mental health and substance abuse treatment records. Generally, this type of information is confidential. Instruct the caseworkers to ask parents to sign release of information forms to help them obtain the records. If the parent refuses, you should, at an initial hearing, request a court order for the caseworker to get these records.[8]

Be familiar with your state's case law because in some places the court cannot issue such an order until the judge has made an adjudication that the child was abused or neglected.

***Ensure Case Plans Are Honest With Parents*** — Consider suggesting to agency administrators that they add warnings to parents that are attached to all documents, such as initial letters and case plans. Provide them with suggested language for the warning. For example, the Oklahoma legislature mandated that the following language be added to the individual treatment and service plan:

> *To the parent: this is a very important document. Its purpose is to help you provide your child with a safe home within the reasonable period specified in the plan. If you are unwilling or unable to provide your child*

*Consider talking with the agency administration about ways to improve service delivery for parents.*

*with a safe home, your parental and custodial duties and rights may be restricted or terminated or your child may not be returned to you.*[9]

This or similar language might be appropriate for your agency.

***Service Delivery*** — Because ASFA shortens the timeframes for permanency planning, the agency must provide the parents with appropriate services in a timely manner. While resources are often scarce and waiting lists long, it is unfair to expect a parent to accomplish all of the agency objectives without assistance.

Consider talking with the agency administration about ways to improve service delivery for parents. You or someone from the agency could convene a group of service providers in your community, including mental health and substance abuse professionals, housing authority staff, and parenting class coordinators, to discuss service delivery problems. With all the interested players at the table, it may be possible to rework the service system.

***Identify Cases for Concurrent Planning*** — While some agencies have used concurrent planning for many years, others have not used this type of case planning. ASFA specifically allows reasonable efforts to find a permanent situation for a child be made concurrently with reasonable efforts to reunify the birth family.[10] Concurrent planning could include a number of principles such as:

- ❑ honesty with parents about possible results of noncompliance from the beginning of a case while providing reunification services
- ❑ consideration of placing siblings in the same foster home at the initial placement
- ❑ increased recruitment of foster/adopt parents
- ❑ training foster parents to act as mentors for the natural parents and encouraging a relationship between them
- ❑ placing children on adoption exchanges early
- ❑ documenting steps to locate permanent homes for the child

As part of your efforts to help the agency comply with ASFA, you could sit on a committee that reviews cases to determine whether a concurrent plan should be implemented. This approach is used in Washington and the caseworkers have found that these meetings help reduce the time the child remains in foster care. Being familiar with the state legislation, you can advise whether the case is ready for a termination of parental rights petition or another permanent plan.[11]

***Assess Staff Needs*** — ASFA's requirements may add a heavy burden on staff by: shortening timeframes, emphasizing documentation, increasing termination of parental rights petitions, raising the number of children who will need adoptive homes, improving service delivery, expanding the substance

*For ASFA to be implemented well, you and the agency may need to increase your staff.*

and frequency of court hearings and increasing case meetings.

Decide with the agency administration what direction an expansion of staff should take. You can strategize together on ways to gather the resources to hire both agency staff and new attorneys. Remember the Title IV-E funds in addition to funding from other sources may be available to pay attorney salaries.[12] Keep in mind that with adequate staffing, children will be moved to permanent placements in a timely fashion, therefore decreasing foster care costs. Allocating money to hire staff will save money in the future, help the agency comply with ASFA and avoid penalties, and most importantly help children achieve permanence.

### Agency Attorney as Instigator of Change

The spirit of ASFA is about positive change for children, and you are indispensable in making it happen. There are several necessary systemic changes that depend on your active participation.

***When Reasonable Efforts to Reunify the Family are Not Required*** — In most places, the idea of having some cases proceed directly to permanency planning without making reasonable efforts to reunify the family is brand new. In these jurisdictions, the court, agency and attorneys practicing in the system need to develop protocols concerning decision-making in this group of cases. You should be involved in the decision-making. Several issues will need to be addressed:

***(1) At what point in the proceedings does the issue get raised to the court?*** As courts look at this question, they may reach different answers. For example, in Oklahoma, juries handle adjudicatory hearings, and judges are uncomfortable deciding that reasonable efforts to reunify the family are not needed before the jury determines whether the child is dependent or deprived. Therefore, they may choose to wait until the disposition hearing to address the question. Other jurisdictions may decide it is appropriate to examine the issue during the first removal hearing or at an adjudicatory stage. It is important to discuss the issue and reach a consistent conclusion.

***(2) Who raises the issue?*** Again there may not be a uniform answer throughout the country but each jurisdiction should have a protocol. Often, you and the caseworker will have the most relevant and up-to-date information about the family. It seems appropriate, then, that in most cases where not making reunification efforts is an issue, you would raise it to the court. Additionally, the child's attorney should be given latitude to raise the issue for discussion.

In some places, the working group may decide that the judge will raise the question in all cases and ask for information about whether the case is ripe for this examination. The decision to not make reasonable efforts to reunify a family will be made in the minority of cases. However, in the appropriate case it will be an effective tool to move the case efficiently. Therefore, it is necessary to raise the issue in all cases that meet your state's definition of aggravated circumstances.

***(3) How will the issue be handled once it is raised?*** By making the decision not to attempt reunification efforts, the judge is generally saying there is no hope for the parents and the child should be moved into a permanent situation. This is a drastic step and should be considered carefully. The question of the type of hearing to hold and the burden of proof to use is complex. No one wants to deny parents due process or give up on families prematurely. However, ASFA requires a permanency hearing 30 days after this decision is reached. No one wants repetitive hearings that hold up the process. Since ASFA is about moving children into permanent situations in a timely fashion, many drawn-out hearings are inappropriate.

***(4) Whether to combine hearings?*** When making decisions about the hearing process, consider whether your state statute allows you to combine hearings. If so, you may be able to combine the reasonable efforts decision with the permanency hearing or the permanency hearing with the termination of parental rights hearing, if termination is the route you are taking. Another solution is to incorporate testimony from the first hearing into the permanency hearing. When considering this issue, balance the parents' rights with the child's right to a timely decision and develop a system that works in your court.

***Coordinating Agency Reports with Court Findings*** — ASFA requires that all hearings, especially the permanency hearing, be thorough and substantive. The court should be provided in-depth information about the child, the parents' progress, the plan for the family, and the steps underway to complete the plan. One way to assist the court in this process is to ensure the caseworker's report contains all relevant information and is on a computer disk in a format that is consistent with the judge's order. If the court has computer access, the judge can review the report, make changes on the computer and print out an order. The benefit of this plan is all parties leave the courtroom with a consistent order. They know what needs to be done and will not have to hold up the process waiting for an order.[13]

Even if your jurisdiction is not technologically ready to have orders printed from the courtroom, helping the agency provide substantive, concrete reports to the court is a large step. If the court is comfortable with the report, and its structure, it may be more willing to grant the agency's requests in the hearing.

To implement this plan, you can work with the court and the agency to coordinate the effort. By bringing your chief judge and agency administration together in a nonconfrontational meeting, much can be accomplished.

***Notice of Hearings*** — ASFA requires that foster parents, relatives caring for children and preadoptive parents be notified of hearings and the opportunity to be heard.[14] This requirement does not grant these individuals party status, but it does raise a large administrative issue. Since ASFA does not dictate who should be giving the notice, your working group must decide.

In some jurisdictions, the agency must send the notice. In other places, the court sends the notice, but the agency is responsible for making sure the court has the caregiver's correct address. Some states have addressed this issue in new legislation, so be aware of your law. This requirement could become costly and time-consuming.

As the agency representative, you must be aware of the burden the mandate will add to the agency and represent the agency accordingly. With your help, a workable system can be devised.

### Agency Attorney as Ethicist

ASFA is a positive step in helping children reach permanency quickly. However, you should be aware of some potential conflicts and dilemmas.

***Creating Legal Orphans*** — While ASFA speaks to all permanent goals, if a child cannot safely return home and is not residing with a relative, adoption is the preferred plan. As you know, many children are now free for adoption who have not yet been placed in adoptive homes. By decreasing timeframes for filing termination of parental rights petitions, many more children will be in this "freed" status. It is therefore essential that agencies increase recruitment efforts for adoptive families.

Because many children are adopted by their foster parents, it is also important that agencies try to improve their process for helping foster parents become adoptive parents. Permanency planning efforts should begin early in cases to increase the chance that the child will not have to be moved from a family to whom he or she has become attached.

Even with these efforts, there may be times when you must decide whether it is appropriate to try to terminate parental rights when there is no realistic likelihood of locating an adoptive family. There is no easy answer to this issue, but it is one you should explore. In such a case, talk to the caseworker and adoption specialist to find out what steps have already been made to find an adoptive home for the child. Honestly discuss the child's chances for adoption, as well as the agency's track record at placing similar children in adoptive homes. While

*Because many children are adopted by their foster parents, it is also important that agencies try to improve their process for helping foster parents become adoptive parents.*

almost every child is "adoptable," some children have better chances than others. Also, try to find out if the child wants to be adopted and what type of bond exists between the child and the parent.

There is no golden rule to follow in resolving this dilemma. The decision to file a petition must be made on a case-by-case basis and in consultation with the caseworker, adoption specialist, the child's attorney and the child (if he or she is old enough to understand and voice an opinion). This is an issue, though, to consider when making plans that are in the child's best interests.

### Conflict with Agency

Another potential conflict is when the caseworker wants you to file a termination of parental rights petition and you have concerns that appropriate services were not offered to the parents in a timely fashion. As discussed above, part of due process and fairness is helping the parents access the services necessary for them to work towards reunification. Not providing reunification services is one of the exceptions to when ASFA mandates a termination petition be filed.

While resolving this type of dispute must also be done on a case-by-case basis, it helps to have a conflict resolution system set up before the issues arise. For instance, you and the caseworker should talk to your respective supervisors and go up the chain of command to reach a mutually agreeable decision. You should not take action that you believe is ethically unsound; however, some decisions are social work decisions and should be made by the caseworker and supervisor.[15]

## When Reasonable Efforts to Provide Reunification Services are Not Required

### Potential Scenario

Ms. Smith has just given birth to her fourth child. The hospital called the agency because they were aware of Ms. Smith's history. The agency obtained an order to take the newborn child into custody. The agency has the older three siblings in custody and has worked with Ms. Smith for several years. Unfortunately, Ms. Smith suffers from schizophrenia, paranoid type, and has been on and off her medication repeatedly. Ms. Smith was unable to care for the older children and her visitation has been inconsistent. All four children have the same father, Mr. Taylor. Mr. Taylor is mentally limited and has faded in and out of the older children's lives.

You have filed termination of parental rights petitions against both parents for the three other children and the hearing was pending at the time of the fourth child's birth. Is this case appropriate for a judicial finding that reunification efforts do not need to be made? What could the process involve?

### Possible Process to Resolve the Issue

After the agency obtained the order to place the new baby, they should call you and let you know the date of the initial hearing. You could instruct them to gather whatever records they have about the parents' disabilities and about their history while the older children have been in care. If possible, the caseworker can get any new records about the parents' treatment. This may be difficult without a court order. If the parents are already represented because of the court involvement of the older children, consider contacting their attorneys. Notify them that you will be requesting a judicial determination that the agency will not need to make reunification efforts for the new baby.

At the hearing, you should raise the question to the judge. The judge may believe the issue is premature, either because there was not a lot of notice to counsel, no counsel had yet been appointed, all records had not yet been ordered or because the court wants to wait until an adjudicatory finding. Nonetheless, by raising the question, you have placed all parties on notice that you will be pursuing this process.

At whatever hearing you explore the issue, be prepared to present testimony and records for the judge to consider. Also be prepared to discuss the details of ASFA if the judge has questions about the law. Resolving the question may involve a full hearing, but if the judge makes the determination that you are seeking, request that the testimony then be incorporated into the permanency hearing 30 days later. In this type of case, you may be able to file the termination petition quickly, and combine the hearing with that of the siblings. Remember, ASFA's intent is to make the process efficient, not to drag the case out indefinitely. Be creative and perhaps the court and the other parties will follow.

## CONCLUSION

This is an exciting time in child welfare. There is potential for a great deal of good to come from Congress' attempt to make children and their safety a priority. Without question, implementing both the language and the spirit of ASFA will be difficult. Changes may be needed at all levels of your system — from the agency, to your representation and the representation that parents and children receive, to the court and its administration.

You are indispensable to this process and while you cannot do it all on your own, without your energy and input, the children in your community will not receive the benefit that ASFA could afford.

## ENDNOTES

1. ASFA § 101(a), 42 U.S.C. § 671(a)(15)(A).

2. 142 Cong. Rec. § 5710-01 (daily ed. June 4, 1996) (statement of Sen. DeWine).

3. Ibid, 42 U.S.C. § 671 (a)(15)(D).

4. Ibid, 42 U.S.C. § 671 (a)(15)(E).

5. ASFA § 302, 42 U.S.C. § 675(5)(C).

6. ASFA § 103, 42 U.S.C. § 675(5)(E).

7. ASFA § 101, 42 U.S.C. § 671(a)(15)(C).

8. Bussiere, Alice, Abigail English, & Catherine Teare. *Sharing Information: A Guide to Federal Laws on Confidentiality and Disclosure of Information for Child Welfare Agencies.* Washington D.C.: American Bar Association, 1997, 19-24.

9. Oklahoma Enrolled Senate Bill No. 1224. Enacted June 11, 1998.

10. ASFA § 101, 42 U.S.C. § 671 (a)(15)(F).

11. Telephone interview with Linda Katz, MSW, adjunct faculty at the University of Washington School of Social Work, Seattle, Washington, July 14, 1998.

12. Segal, Ellen C. *Evaluating and Improving Child Welfare Agency Legal Representation Self-Assessment Instrument and Commentary.* Washington, D.C.: National Legal Resource Center for Child Advocacy and Protection, American Bar Association, 1988, 58-61.

13. This protocol used by Judge Patricia Macias, 65th Judicial District, Child Welfare Court, El Paso, TX.

14. ASFA § 104, 42 U.S.C. § 675(5)(G).

15. Laver, Mimi. "Agency Attorneys and Caseworkers: Working Well Together." *Child Law Practice* 17(7), September 1998.

APPENDIX A

# In The Workplace: The Cost of Caring: Burnout

*by Katherine Trinidad*

Attorneys in the child welfare field face demanding expectations, high caseloads and constant stress. These conditions are well-recognized as part of the job. But if not handled properly, they can cause more than just a headache.

Burnout is an issue of particular concern for occupations where the relationship between providers and recipients is central to the job and where providing service can be highly emotional. Burnout symptoms, such as fatigue and disengagement, are easy to identify, but more difficult to treat.

In the past, the legal world was slow to acknowledge burnout, fearing it would chip away at the profession's tough veneer. Many lawyers ignored the problem because admitting its symptoms was seen as a sign of weakness.

A growing amount of research on burnout has led to a greater acceptance of it as a legitimate concern for the legal world. According to a survey the ABA Young Lawyers Section conducted of more than 2,000 lawyers in 1995, nearly 30% were dissatisfied with their careers. The survey found that to a great extent lawyers linked their career dissatisfaction to increased levels of mental and physical stress.[1] With

*In the past, the legal world was slow to acknowledge burnout, fearing it would chip away at the profession's tough veneer.*

increased attention to the problem, attitudes are changing, and more resources are available to help lawyers successfully cope with the daily, on-the-job burn.

## BEATING BURNOUT

If a burned-out person is like a car whose battery has died, then how can you recharge the battery? In addition to a law degree, Dennis Kozich holds a Ph.D. in counseling, and offers some valuable advice. Each individual has to devise a personalized plan to deal with job stress and frustration. Kozich suggests achieving the elusive "balance" in life. "Find something you like to do that has nothing to do with your head. Imagine it was cut off and thrown away and let your gut make the decisions." This balance is only impossible to achieve for those whose goals and values are undefined. Kozich compares these people to hamsters on a treadmill who think they only need to run faster to get by.

### Set realistic goals

Beware the "superhuman" complex, and know your limitations as a person and as a lawyer. The demands of working with maltreated children are great. In a field in which professional expectations go beyond knowing the law to understanding child development, family dynamics and how to interact with children, you may often feel pressure to be all things to all people. Give your own and professional expectations a reality check. Assess your priorities and what you can realistically accomplish in each situation.

### Share the load

Find two or three other attorneys in your community who are willing to take on cases for you and vice versa. This can be an invaluable resource either when you have too much to juggle or when you simply need to get away. Also, be sure to delegate work to any support staff who can help with the burden.

### Develop a support network

Join a professional association and/or form a support group. Reach out to colleagues from the wide field of child welfare: lawyers, judges, social workers, mental health professionals and others. A strong support network can provide not only an attentive ear, but also an understanding heart. Also, collaboration among these professional disciplines can only improve service to children.

### Contact your local lawyer assistance program

Help is available through many state and local bar association lawyer assistance programs. These programs provide confidential counseling services to those who call their helplines. For more information on assistance programs in your state, contact the ABA Center for Professional Services at 312/988-5359.

*"Find something you like to do that has nothing to do with your head. Imagine it was cut off and thrown away and let your gut make the decisions."*

### Take advantage of educational opportunities

Sometimes lack of knowledge in certain areas can contribute to stress and feelings of inadequacy. Refresher courses in trial skills, new laws and their impact on your practice, and other areas can give you the tools to do your job with confidence. Educational opportunities are available through training sessions, CLE courses, and conferences. These programs are also ideal settings to form relationships with other advocates who can provide support and advice.

For more information on CLE programs, contact the ABA Service Center at 800/285-2221. Local law schools and bar associations may also offer CLE programs. The ABA Center on Children and the Law (202/662-1720) holds a biannual conference, and the National Association of Counsel for Children (888/828-NACC) offers an annual conference for child advocates.

### Evaluate your commitment to child advocacy: Is it right for you?

Some newcomers to child law take happily to their jobs, while others flounder as they realize they have made a mistake. In order to avoid the latter situation and/or future burnout, therapists and experienced lawyers suggest evaluating your dedication, motivation and stamina to work in child advocacy. The important questions:

- ❑ Are you committed to public service?
- ❑ How important is a lucrative career to you?
- ❑ Are you comfortable interacting with children?
- ❑ Are you easily frustrated by bureaucracies?
- ❑ Can you manage a high caseload?
- ❑ Do you have time to take care of your personal needs?

*If you find that you are unable to function effectively at work or at home, consider taking some time off...*

### Find the right fit

Evaluate yourself and the quality of your work and life. Are you in the best job situation for you and your clients? Many front-line child welfare attorneys choose to stay in the field by developing other talents and skills. Consider other areas within the field such as teaching, consulting or policy work.

### Learn to laugh

Child welfare work can be a sobering and emotionally-draining experience. A sense of humor plays a valuable role in releasing some of the daily tension and stress. Of course, humor has a proper time and place. For example, you can tell a funny story to a child client to help him or her relax. You can also look for the absurdity in certain situations or simply laugh at yourself. (And don't forget to laugh at the judge's jokes.)

### Make time for yourself

Although your schedule may be tight, allow some time to take care of yourself. Exercising regularly and eating well can help your physical health. But, do not neglect your emotional well-being. Evaluate your state of mind regularly and do not allow problems to fester. If you find that you are unable to function effectively at work or at home, consider taking some time off — a vacation, or a sabbatical.

### Pursue other interests

Find sources of enjoyment and diversion away from your professional world. Focusing on your personal happiness can also affect your professional satisfaction. Outside interests can refresh your outlook and even improve the quality of your work.

### Elevate the field

While it is important to focus on preventing and treating burnout, it may be more important to work on elevating the status of the child law field. Many lawyers still battle the perception of child-related law as "kiddie-court," issues surrounding prestige, and disproportionate pay.

Marvin Ventrell, who represented children for 8 years before becoming executive director of the National Association of Counsel for Children (NACC), believes there is a direct connection between burnout and professional status and pay. "It is fundamentally wrong to require professionals to perform such skilled, important work for society and fail to reward them proportionately in terms of status and pay. While money may not buy happiness or eliminate stress, we need to recognize the connection, get past the notion that 'do gooders' need to be poor, and work to improve our professional condition."

Ventrell agrees that the problem of burnout should be monitored and treated. He emphasizes, however, the problem of lack of professional status and the need to raise the profession to another level. The NACC is available to help child advocates deal with practice issues including burnout. For more information, contact the NACC National Child Advocacy Resource Center at 888/828-NACC.

### The Role of Law Schools

Some law schools encourage students to evaluate their commitment to child advocacy before they begin practicing. Schools with established child law programs are usually more successful in this endeavor. Fortunately, the number of schools incorporating these specialized programs is growing. According to a 1996 report by the ABA Section of Litigation Task Force on Children, at least 38 law schools now offer child advocacy programs.[2]

### Preparing Advocates for Life on the Front Lines

At Loyola University Chicago School of Law, the interdisciplinary curriculum for child law students includes elements to prepare them for an often overwhelming profession. Course work and readings highlight the pressures and obstacles that can be expected. Students are required to participate in two "hands-on" internships. In addition, mental health experts are brought in to help students explore issues such as "compassion fatigue" and stress management. Students examine the effects of stress on themselves, on their decision-making and on their relationships with children.

Former Director of Loyola's Civitas Childlaw Center Richard Cozzola says law schools need to give students the opportunity to address these issues in the classroom so that they can be effective advocates in the courtroom. Loyola students are also taking responsibility for their current and future well-being by forming a child law support group.

More law schools would do well to follow the CIVITAS program's lead. Anna Davis, 24, is a third-year law student at the University of Oregon, where no child law program exists. According to Davis, the level of preparation for an advocacy career has been minimal. Neither her course work nor her professors have addressed issues such as dealing with cases on an emotional level, managing stress or balancing your work and personal life.

In the last couple of years, Davis has tried to fill the gap in her education through internships which exposed her not only to the daily grind, but also to attorneys eager to advise and counsel. Davis plans to become a trial attorney working for abused and delinquent children. She is aware of the profession's pitfalls and pressures, and is concerned about succumbing to burnout. “But,” she adds, “this is a job where I can make a difference and that will push me to wake up every day, go out there and never give up.”

## CONCLUSION

In many cases, burnout does not push its victims out of the child advocacy field entirely. Instead it often leads to a reevaluation and reassessment of one's coping mechanisms and stress management skills. Fortunately, concerted efforts on the part of individuals, organizations and schools are being made to ensure the path of child advocates becomes a little easier to travel.

## HELPFUL BOOKS

Cherniss, Cary. *Beyond Burnout: How Teachers, Nurses, Therapists, and Lawyers Recover from Stress and Disillusionment.* Routledge, 1995. $18.95. To order: 800/634-7064.

Figley, Charles R., ed. *Compassion Fatigue.* New York: Brunner/Mazel Publishers, 1995. $37.95. To order: 212/924-3344.

Portnoy, Dennis. *Overextended and Undernourished: A Self-Care Guide for People in Helping Roles.* Johnson Institute, 1996. $5.95.

Ross, Richard. *A Day in Part 15: Law & Order in Family Court.* New York: Four Walls Eight Windows, 1997. $22. To order: 800/626-4848.

Tamminen, Julie M., ed. *Living with the Law: Strategies to Avoid Burnout and Create Balance.* Chicago: American Bar Association, 1996. $69.96. To order: 800/285-2221.

## ENDNOTES

1. ABA Young Lawyers Division, ABA Young Lawyers Division Survey. American Bar Association, 1995.

2. ABA Section of Litigation Task Force on Children. A Directory of Pro Bono Children's Law Programs, 3d ed. Chicago: American Bar Association, June 1996.

APPENDIX B:

# Websites You Might Visit

## American Bar Association Center on Children and the Law

**www.abanet.org/child**
[links to ABA entities such as Commission on Domestic Violence, Commission on Mental and Physical Disability Law, Family Law Section, Juvenile Justice Center, Litigation Section Task Force on Children, and Steering Committee on the Unmet Legal Needs of Children]

## National Association of Counsel for Children

**www.NACCchildlaw.org**

## National CASA Association

**www.nationalcasa.org**

## National Clearinghouse on Child Abuse and Neglect Information

**www.calib.com/nccanch/index.htm**

## National Conference of State Legislatures

**www.ncsl.org/programs/cyf/cw.htm**

## National Council of Juvenile and Family Court Judges

**www.ncjfcj.unr.edu**
[link to National Center for Juvenile Justice]

## Child Welfare League of America

**www.cwla.org**

## Children's Defense Fund

**www.childrensdefense.org**

### FamLawLit-survey of current family law periodical literature

**www.divorcenet.com/familylaw/famlaw02.html**

### State Justice Institute

**www.clark.net/pub/sji/**

### National Center for State Courts

**www.ncsc.dni.us**

### National Criminal Justice Reference Service

**www.ncjrs.org**

[Link to USDOJ Office of Juvenile Justice and Delinquency Prevention]

## CHILD DEVELOPMENTAL/SPECIAL NEEDS

### USHHS Maternal and Child Health Bureau

**www.os.dhhs.gov/hrsa/mchb**

[link to child abuse and adolescent health; school health; special health care needs]

### Medline

**www.nim.nih.gov**

### National Institute of Health

**www.nih.gov**

### National Institute of Mental Health

**www.nimh.nih.gov**

### National Association of Protection and Advocacy Systems

**www.protectionandadvocacy.com**

### National Mental Health Association

**www.nmha.org**

## Handsnet

**www.handsnet.org**
[national nonprofit that manages online networking linking 5,000 public interest and human services groups; free 30-day trial membership, then subscription fee]

## National Adolescent Health Information Center

[website being developed]

University of California, San Francisco

School of Medicine

Department of Pediatrics

Division of Adolescent Medicine

1388 Sutter Street, Suite 605-A

San Francisco, CA 94109

(415) 502-4856

E-Mail: nahic@itsa.ucsf.edu

## American Medical Association

**www.ama-assn.org**
[Link to Medical Science and Education and Adolescent Health On-Line]

## American Psychological Association

**www.apa.org**

## American Psychiatric Asssociation

**www.psych.org**

## American Academy of Child and Adolescent Psychiatry

**www.aacap.org**

## UCLA Center for Mental Health in Schools

**www.lifesci.ucla.edu/psych/mh/**

## National Association of Social Workers

**www.naswdc.org**

APPENDIX C:

# Helpful Forms

## CHILD DEPENDENCY UNIT OFFICE OF THE COUNTY COUNSEL, SANTA CLARA COUNTY

## JOB DESCRIPTION

The Child Dependency Unit (CDU) of the Santa Clara County Office of the County Counsel represents the Department of Family and Children's Services (DFCS) in Welfare and Institutions Code § 300 dependency (child abuse and neglect) proceedings in juvenile court. The Santa Clara County juvenile dependency court operates three daily calendar departments on a full-time basis and sends contested hearings with a time estimate exceeding one day to the master civil trial calendar in the Superior Court. The juvenile court also sponsors a dependency mediation program that conducts approximately five half-day sessions per week. The juvenile court supervises approximately 3500-4000 dependent children at any given time. The juvenile dependency court conducts approximately 10,000 hearings per year.

As required by law, CDU deputies appear on behalf of DFCS at every hearing, every mediation and every trial conducted by the juvenile dependency court. CDU deputies serve in a quasi-prosecutorial role as DFCS by law bears the burden of proof and production of evidence at most hearings in juvenile dependency court. CDU deputies provide social workers with summary memos following every court hearings. CDU deputies represent DFCS in all writ and appeal proceedings which arise from dependency hearings. CDU deputies provide daily telephone advice and twice-weekly on-site advice for the three-hundred-plus child welfare social worker at DFCS. CDU deputies are normally responsible for drafting orders and judgments after contested hearings. CDU court assistants and support staff (including legal secretaries, clerks, and receptions) are responsible for distributing copies of social workers' court reports and memorandums to the court and attorneys. CDU court assistants and support staff are responsible for arranging for the transportation of incarcerated parents, arranging for the availability of interpreters, mailing all notices for regular hearings, subpoenaing witnesses, presenting DFCS ex parte applications to the court, and preparing and serving special notices in proceedings to terminate parental rights.

In addition to their courtroom duties, CDU deputies, at the request of DFCS and the Presiding Judge, also participate in numerous dependency system-related meetings, including the Presiding Judge's Dependency System Coordinating Committee, the Drug Court Committee, the Permanency Planning Committee, the Court Advocate Steering Committee, the Initial Hearing Committee, the Domestic Violence Council, the Tri-Court Committee (Family, Probate and Juvenile Courts), the Multi-Disciplinary Child Interview Steering Committee, the Dependency Mediation Committee, the Forensic Human Services Certificate Program Executive Committee, the Supreme Court's Year 2020 Task Force, and numerous seminars and conference sponsored by the Department.

CDU deputies also perform special projects for DFCS such as revising the court report recommendation formats, developing procedures for implementing significant changes in the law, and reviewing and revising the Court Services Handbook. CDU deputies assist the Department in obtaining Standing Orders from the Superior Court to facilitate the exchange of information and the placement of foster children. CDU deputies periodically assist with drafting revisions to the Local and State Rules of Court which govern dependency proceedings. CDU deputies also assist the Department in complying with state and federal statutory and appellate law to avoid legal liabilities and facilitate eligibility for state and federal reimbursements. CDU deputies review proposed state and federal legislation and advise the Department with respect to the impact of the legislation on cases and the day-to-day operation of the Department. On occasion CDU deputies are asked to assist in drafting child welfare legislation.

CDU deputies also provide forensic training for the Juvenile Court mediators and for the Family Group Conference Facilitators. CDU deputies are also frequently asked to provide training at seminars and conferences sponsored by the Department, by the State Association of County Counsels, and by the State Judicial Council.

# BROWN BAG LUNCH SEMINARS

## SANTA CLARA DEPARTMENT OF FAMILY & CHILDREN'S SERVICES

| DATE | TOPIC | ATTORNEY |
|---|---|---|
| 3/18/98 | 1998 Legislative Changes: Dependency Proceedings | Clark |
| 4/23/98 | How to persuade the court to dismiss your case | Bennett |
| 5/28/98 | Reasonable services for incarcerated or difficult clients | Clark |
| 6/25/99 | How to prepare to testify as an expert witness | Robinson |
| 7/23/98 | How to prepare for a reasonable efforts/services trial | Heggie/ Rossi |
| 8/27/98 | When to consider a reunification bypass | Burland |
| 9/24/98 | Preparing "family court" custody orders | Hogan |
| 10/22/98 | How to prepare for a termination of parental rights trial | Beglau/Warsaw |
| 11/19/98* | Indian Child Welfare Act | Bennett |
| 12/17/98* | How to prove your 342/387/388 petition | Robinson |

## 1999 Topics:

- ❑ Assessing potential relatives per 361.3
- ❑ Choosing the right recommendations for your court report
- ❑ Responding to discovery requests
- ❑ Recent developments in dependency appellate law
- ❑ How to read a rap sheet
- ❑ How to avoid the courtroom and still succeed
- ❑ Paternity Issues

Each seminar is scheduled for one hour (45 minute presentation, 15 minutes for questions). Please distribute a written outline and materials. The seminars are scheduled for the fourth Thursday of each month unless otherwise noted by an *. The seminars will be held in the California room at 1725 Technology Drive. The department will audiotape the seminars. Judy Bushey is our liaison (x5699)

# Offsite Program

**SANTA CLARA COUNTY SOCIAL SERVICES AGENCY
DEPARTMENT OF FAMILY AND CHILDREN'S SERVICES
MANAGER, SUPERVISOR, AND COUNTY COUNSEL**

**Friday, February 12, 1999
8:00AM - 1:30PM, Wyndham Hotel**

| | |
|---|---|
| 8:00 AM - 8:30AM | Arrival/ Coffee |
| 8:30 AM - 8:40 AM | Welcome - L.Martin/ D. Bennett/ M. Clark |
| 8:40 AM - 9:00 AM | Opening Remarks/ DFCS Philosophy - Leroy Martin |
| 9:00 AM - 10:15AM | Common strategies for managing case crises/ working effectively as a team |

**Large Group:**

1. Who does county counsel represent and what is county counsel's role?

2. What is the changing role of the DFCS supervisor and manager?

**Break Out Groups:**

3. Dealing with hostile judicial officers/ clarifying the limits of our mandate: SWS/DFCS Management / County Counsel

4. Common strategies for presenting ourselves in court in complex situations, i.e., non-petitioned sibling cases; newborn, siblings in out of home care; intra-bureaucratic conflicts, etc.

5. Uncovered caseloads: supervision, court reports, court appearance, recruitment

**Large Group:**

6. The value of encouragement/ affirmation

| | |
|---|---|
| 10:15 AM- 10:30 AM | Break |
| 10:30 AM - 12:00 PM | Legal and Service Trends for Child Welfare |

**A. Legal Trends**

More trials and writs/appeals; services to incarcerated parents; sibling contact; concurrent planning: new reunification time lines, emphasis on TPR, and considering return to parent at post-pph; rights of foster parents; education needs of dependents; search warrants; Initial Court Hearing

**B. Service Trends ( Approximately 3 minutes per topic)**

Regionalization - Leroy Martin

Risk Assessment - Gwen Westphal

Permanency Planning/
Concurrent Planning - Frances Munroe, Maria Nasjleti

Family Conferencing - Kris Fisher

Wraparound Services - Brad Norman

System of Care - Brad Norman

Shelter Realities - Linda Carpenter

CalWorks - Lisle Cohen

Drug Court - Frances Munroe

Informal Supervision - Hortencia Calvillo

12:00 PM - 12:30 PM **Where Do We Go From Here?**

Committees, county counsel meetings with units, managers/supervisors/ county counsel quarterly meetings, etc.?

12:30 PM - 1:30 PM Lunch

# Forensic Human Services

**A Certificate Program for Human Service Professionals–Santa Clara County**

Program Brochure

A Joint Program

College of Social Work

San Jose State University

Child Welfare Training Institute

Santa Clara County Social Services Agency

Santa Clara County Office of the County Counsel

Santa Clara County Superior Court

## PROGRAM OVERVIEW

Human service professionals are increasingly called upon to provide information and recommendations to the court.

Knowledge and understanding of the court process are often essential to the achievement of ultimate case goals.

The Forensic Human Services Certificate Program is designed to prepare human service professionals to effectively present their clinical knowledge and opinions in a forensic setting.

The College of Social Work at San Jose State University and the Child Welfare Training Institute of Santa Clara County Social Service Agency jointly recognize the increasing need for human service professionals, particularly those working in the area of child welfare, to have specialized forensic knowledge and skill.

The program sponsors, in cooperation with the Santa Clara County Superior Court and Office of County Counsel, have combined their resources to develop and sponsor a course of study leading to a Diploma in Forensic Human Services.

Students who participate in the program will receive a certificate for each course completed. Students who complete the entire program will be awarded a Diploma in Forensic Human Services.

For more information, please call Karrie Chatigny at (408) 999-6151

## PROFESSIONAL VALUE

The program responds to the ever increasing need for human service professionals to understand legal requirements and the court process as they impact children and families.

A Diploma in Forensic Human Services will enhance the reputation and credibility of a human service professional testifying as an expert witness.

While most participants hold master's degree or greater, the program assumes a minimum educational level of a bachelor's degree.

## COURSES

This specialized training program consists of 150 hours of classroom instruction. The program consists of courses which address the following subjects:

1. Introduction to Judicial Process (20 hours)
2. Juvenile Court Law (20 hours)
3. Collecting Information (30 hours)
4. Child Protection in a Family Preservation Context (20 hours)
5. Writing Court Reports and Other Forensic Documents (30 hours)
6. Preparing and Presenting Testimony (30 hours)

The courses are scheduled to accommodate the working professional.

Participants should be able to successfully participate in class sessions and complete outside assignments while maintaining full time employment.

The courses are designed to taken in the prescribed sequence. However participants may take the courses in the order that best meets their scheduling needs.

Although participants must complete all six courses to receive their Diploma in Forensic Human Service, each course is self-contained and can be taken separately. Individual certificates will be awarded for successful completion of each course.

Each course requires a minimum of 14 participants.

Outside agencies and departments can arrange with the executive committee for condensed, on-site training seminars that address each of the courses listed and/or related topics. For further information about on-site seminars, please contact L. Michael Clark at (408)-299-4280.

## CONTINUING EDUCATION CREDIT

All courses are eligible for National Association of Social Workers (NASW) Continuing Education Units (CEU's) on a unit-for-hour basis. Provider Number 96-116.

* NOTE: C.E.U.'s subject to 1997 NASW Approval of Continuing Providership.

The courses described in this brochure may be eligible for Peace Officer Standard and Training (P.O.S.T.) training points.

## ATTENDANCE POLICY

In order to receive credit for a course, a student is expected to attend all class sessions. However, up to two excused absences are permitted for each course. The instructor must be notified in advance of any absences. If for extenuating reasons a student misses more than two classes, the student must obtain approval from the executive committee in order to receive credit for the course.

Students are expected` to be on time for each class, to return from breaks in a timely fashion, and to remain in class until the end of each session. Any serious deviation from this policy may result in no credit being given for class.

## COMPLETION OF WORK

All course assignments must be completed by the assigned due date unless otherwise arranged in advance with the instructor.

## GRADING

Courses are graded on a pass/fail basis

## AUDIT POLICY

Individuals may audit any course. The fee for auditing a course will be the same as the fee for taking the course for credit. However, college student interns may audit any course for $50.00.

Guests may attend one class session for each course at no charge.

## EXCEPTIONS

Requests for exceptions to these policies may be presented to the executive committee by letter.

## REGISTRATION INFORMATION

Fees for each course are listed on the attached registration form. Register by returning a complete photo static copy of the registration form attached and person listed on the registration form. Make checks payable to "Forensics."

## CONFIRMATION

Registration will be confirmed by mail two weeks prior to start date of course.

## REFUNDS

Refunds are available on a limited basis. After the first class meeting, a $25.00 administrative fee will be charged. No refunds will be available after the second class meeting. However, registration fees in future classes may be waived by the Executive Committee to offset paid fees when there are extenuating circumstances.

## DATES AND TIMES

The dates and times for courses will be published by the Agency periodically.

## SCHEDULE CHANGES

The dates and times for courses when published are subject to change, but course content will remain the same.

## LOCATION

All classes will be conducted at the Social Services Agency, 1725 Technology Drive, San Jose. Directions will be sent with confirmations.

## TUITION REIMBURSEMENT

Santa Clara County employees may apply for tuition reimbursement/professional development funds for these courses. Other organizations may also provide similar funding support.

Tuition fees are waived for Santa Clara County DFCS Social Workers and Supervisors.

### INFORMATION

For more information, please call Karrie Chatigny at (408) 999-6151.

## COURSE DESCRIPTION

## FHS01 INTRODUCTION TO JUDICIAL PROCESS (20 HOURS)

### DESCRIPTION

This course will provide human service professionals with an overview of the American judicial process in general and the California judicial process in particular.

### COMPETENCIES

After completing this course, participants will be able to:

**Identify and describe:**

- ❑ The fundamental principals of law and procedure that govern the adversarial system of law
- ❑ The primary ethical duties of a lawyer and explain how these duties may potentially conflict with the purpose of an adversary proceeding
- ❑ The competing individual, family and societal interests in human services-related court proceedings
- ❑ The legal roles of the parties and participants in various court proceedings
- ❑ The structure of the California court system

- ❑ Basic courtroom etiquette and protocol

**Compare and contrast:**

- ❑ The legal and clinical models for resolving disputes

**Understand and explain:**

- ❑ How to respond to subpoenas and discovery requests while protecting confidential or privileged information
- ❑ The sanction of contempt of court

**Develop and Describe:**

- ❑ Your own strategy for utilizing the court process to achieve case management goals

**Analyze:**

- ❑ Actual court proceedings

### PARTICIPANT EXPECTATIONS

To successfully complete this course, participants are expected to:

- ❑ Observe five hours of court proceedings
- ❑ Complete assigned reading and participate in class discussions
- ❑ Write a term paper
- ❑ Pass a final examination

## FHSO2 JUVENILE COURT LAW (20 HOURS)

### DESCRIPTION

This course will provide human service professionals with an overview of the juvenile court process, including delinquency, dependency and status offender cases. Primary emphasis will be given to juvenile dependency cases.

## COMPETENCIES

After completing this course, participants will be able to:

### Identify and describe:

- ❑ The various legal actions that can be filed in juvenile court
- ❑ The various types of hearings in juvenile court delinquency and dependency proceedings in terms of due process rights and legal requirements, evidentiary issues, alternative findings and orders, presumptions, burdens of proof and production, investigation and report writing, strategic considerations and settlement options.
- ❑ The various statutory provisions of law which govern the dependency process
- ❑ The various federal and interstate laws which affect juvenile court proceedings

### Compare and contrast:

- ❑ The juvenile court dependency system with the delinquency court system, the adult criminal court system and the family court system in terms of philosophy and structure

## PARTICIPANT EXPECTATIONS

To successfully complete this course, participants are expected to:

- ❑ Complete assigned reading and participate in class discussions
- ❑ Draft a detailed flow chart of the dependency process
- ❑ Pass a final examination

## FHS03 COLLECTING INFORMATION (30 HOURS)

### DESCRIPTION

This course examines methods and techniques for collecting effective, usable, factual information for presentation in judicial proceedings involving abused and neglected children.

### COMPETENCIES

After completing this course, participants will be able to:

**Identify and describe:**

- ❑ The various types of investigations related to child abuse and neglect, the various sources of evidence, the various methods of collecting evidence, the roles of the various information gatherers.
- ❑ Techniques and strategies for interviewing adult witness
- ❑ Techniques and strategies for interviewing child witness, and explain how the developmental stages and special needs of children impact the information gathering process
- ❑ Methods for preserving information, including notetaking, audiotapes, videotapes, and photographs
- ❑ Various obstacles to effective interviewing, including the interviewer

**Demonstrate proficiency in:**

- ❑ Creating a strategic plan for collecting information
- ❑ Interviewing adult and child witnesses

## PARTICIPANT EXPECTATIONS

To successfully complete this course, participants are expected to:

**Create:**

- ❑ An investigation plan based upon a hypothetical set of facts

**Conduct:**

- ❑ A mock videotaped interview of an adult witness and critique the interview
- ❑ A mock videotaped interview of child witness and critique the interview

# FHSO4 CHILD PROTECTION IN A FAMILY PRESERVATION CONTEXT (20 HOURS)

## DESCRIPTION

This course is designed to help human service professionals select and utilize alternative forensic strategies for achieving the goal of child protection. Discussion will include family preservation and reasonable efforts, least restrictive alternative, and the various judicial and non-judicial interventions available to achieve the goal of child protection. Emphasis will be given to the intergration of child protection decision-making with selected family and developmental theories in a forensic context.

## COMPETENCIES

After completing this course, participants will be able to:

**Demonstrate knowledge of:**

- ❑ Various judicial interventions such as emancipation, guardianship, relinquishment,

- dependency with family maintenance, dependency with family reunification and dependency with termination of parental rights
- Various nonjudicial interventions such as voluntary family maintenance, voluntary family reunification and informal supervision

**Demonstrate:**

- An improved ability to select various judicial and nonjudicial interventions for child protection

**Identify and describe:**

- The various federal, state and local mandates affecting the family preservation doctrine

### PARTICIPANT EXPECTATIONS

To successfully complete this course, participants are expected to:

- Participate in class discussion
- Complete class project
- Pass a final examination

## FHS05 WRITING COURT REPORTS AND DOCUMENTS (30 HOURS)

### DESCRIPTION

This course will help participants improve their ability to present facts in court reports. Emphasis will be given to documentation and content that satisfy court requirements.

### COMPETENCIES

After completing this course, participants will be able to:

**Distinguish:**

- ❑ Fact statements from opinion statement and describe methods for weaving facts and opinion statements together
- ❑ Factual language from judgmental language and describe the benefits and liabilities of each

**Identify and describe:**

- ❑ Methods of using a court report to engage clients in services
- ❑ The relationship between court reports and witness credibility

**Demonstrate:**

- ❑ Skill in outlining and summarizing complex fact situation
- ❑ Proficiency in writing an assessment-oriented court report
- ❑ Proficiency in tailoring social work and/or therapeutic interventions with case assessments.

**Describe:**

- ❑ The importance of attachments and addenda to court reports and describe the legal requirements related to the admissibility of attachments and addenda in child welfare cases
- ❑ The concept of constitutional due process as it relates to preparation and dissemination of court reports

## PARTICIPANT EXPECTATIONS

To successfully complete this course, participants are expected to:

**Write:**

- ❑ A factual court report

- ❑ An assessment report oriented towards presentation in court
- ❑ A case plan oriented towards presentation in court

**Complete:**

- ❑ Various short writing assignments in and outside of class

## FHS06 PREPARING AND PRESENTING TESTIMONY (30 HOURS)

### DESCRIPTION

This is an experiential course designed to build and improve the skills that are necessary for clear and effective testimony. The course will teach participants how to prepare to testify, how to effectively utilize legal consultation, and how to enjoy cross-examination. The course will include mandatory participation in videotaped simulation exercises.

### COMPETENCIES

After completing this course, participants will be able to :

**Develop a:**

- ❑ Personal system for preparing their minds and files for trials
- ❑ Curriculum vitae suited for use in the courtroom as an expert witness
- ❑ Personal strategy for maintaining composure and objectivity on the witness stand

**Understand and describe:**

- ❑ The purpose of direct and cross-examination in the context of the adversarial process

- ❑ The importance of, and methods for, establishing credibility in the courtroom
- ❑ The voir dire process as it relates to qualification of an expert witness

**Identify:**

- ❑ Common traps that witnesses fall into and describe strategies for avoiding these traps
- ❑ And describe how the developmental stages of children and their special needs will impact the testimonial process

**Compare and Contrast:**

- ❑ Lay testimony with expert testimony

**Demonstrate:**

- ❑ Proficiency in responding directly, succinctly and effectively to direct and cross-examination questions

## PARTICIPANT EXPECTATIONS

To successfully complete this course, participants are expected to:

**Testify as:**

- ❑ A lay witness in a videotaped mock examination with self and peer critiques
- ❑ An expert witness in a videotaped mock examination with self and peer critique

**Prepare:**

- ❑ A curriculum vitae for use as an expert witness

**Write:**

- ❑ A short paper related to testifying in court

# San Diego County Counsel Paternity Tracking Sheet

Father on birth certificate:_______________ ❑ Copy in file

Father on hospital declaration: ___________ ❑ Copy in file

Father per prior Court orders (describe):_______________

_______________________________________________

_______________________________________________

Dated: ___________ ❑ Copy in file

❑ FSD judgment was entered by default

**Paternity Inquiry** conducted

Copies of Mo's ❑ Fa#1's ❑ Fa#2's ❑

questionnaires in file ❑

❑ Mo, on (date):__________, lists as Fa(s) ______________

❑ Fa#1 ___________on (date): ___________

❑ acknowledges ❑ denies ❑ questions

❑ Fa#2 ___________on (date): ___________

❑ acknowledges ❑ denies ❑ questions

Notes:___________________________________________

_______________________________________________

**316.2** notice given to:

Fa#1 ❑ on (date): __________________

Fa#2 ❑ on (date): __________________

Fa#1 ___________________________ :

Date of Status Finding: _____________,

**Court Finding:** ❑ alleged ❑ presumed ❑ biological

❑ **Paternity testing** ordered on (date): ______________

Requested by: ________

Date of Results: ______________

Fa#1 ❑ excluded ❑ not excluded

Date Court Acts on results:________________

**Presumption basis:**

❑ marriage on (date): _______________ ❑ **conclusive**

❑ received child into home and held child out as his own

Notes:____________________________________________

____________________________________________

**Fa#2**__________________________________________:

Date of Status Finding: _______________,

**Court Finding:** ❑ alleged ❑ presumed ❑ biological

❑ **Paternity testing** ordered on (date):

_________________ Requested by: _________

Date of Results: ______________

Fa#1 ❑ excluded ❑ not excluded

Date Court Acts on results:________________

**Presumption basis:**

❑ marriage on (date): _______________ ❑ **conclusive**

❑ received child into home and held child out as his own

Notes: ____________________________________

____________________________________________

❑ **Paternity judgment** entered as to Fa#1

______________ on (date):___________

❑ **Paternity judgment** entered as to Fa#2

_____________ on (date): ___________

Notes:

____________________________________________

____________________________________________

**Name (child):** ___________________________________

**Date of Birth:** ___________ **CC Case No:**___________

Confidential Attorney Work Product/Non Discoverable

# OFFICE OF COUNTY COUNSEL JUVENILE DEPENDENCY DIVISION

## PERFORMANCE EVALUATION FOR ATTORNEYS

## SECTION A: IDENTIFYING INFORMATION

Appt. Auth.: ________________________________

Department/ Agency Title: ____________________

Social Security No.: _________________________

Class No.: _________________________________

Classification: _____________________________

Employee Name: ____________________________

Reason for Rating:

- ❑ Mid-Probation
- ❑ Final Probation
- ❑ Regular
- ❑ Dept. Originated

If Department originated, state reason such as separation, promotion, demotion, transfer.

__________________________________________

Rating Period

FROM: ____________ TO: ______________

## SECTION B: OVERALL PERFORMANCE RATING

Based on the ratings and comments set forth in this evaluation, this attorney's overall performance during the rating period:

- ❑ Exceeded Performance Standards
- ❑ Met Performance Standards
- ❑ Did Not Meet Performance Standards

(Attach a narrative commenting on attorney's overall performance. Include specific comments on ratings of "Exceeds" or "Does Not Meet" Performance Standards. If the overall performance or any of the separate performance functions did not meet performance standards, the narrative also must include a plan for improvement.)

## SECTION C: RATINGS OF PERFORMANCE FUNCTIONS

### I. DELIVERY OF LEGAL SERVICE

| A. Legal Knowledge | Exceeds Performance Standards | Meets Performance Standards | Does Not Meet Performance Standards |
|---|---|---|---|
| 1. Provides thorough, complete and accurate legal advice | ❑ | ❑ | ❑ |
| 2. Demonstrates thorough knowledge of juvenile dependency law | ❑ | ❑ | ❑ |
| 3. Demonstrates general knowledge of law | ❑ | ❑ | ❑ |
| 4. Demonstrates initiative in expanding scope and depth of legal knowledge | ❑ | ❑ | ❑ |
| 5. Takes advantage of substantive training opportunities from all available sources | ❑ | ❑ | ❑ |

| | Exceeds Performance Standards | Meets Performance Standards | Does Not Meet Performance Standards |
|---|---|---|---|
| **B. Analytical Abilities** | | | |
| 1. Identifies relevant facts | ❑ | ❑ | ❑ |
| 2. Identifies and focus on critical legal issues, including public policy Consideration and County policies | ❑ | ❑ | ❑ |
| 3. Demonstrates good judgment | ❑ | ❑ | ❑ |
| 4. Recognizes the gravity and ramification of issues beyond immediate assignment | ❑ | ❑ | ❑ |
| 5. Analyzes problems thoroughly | ❑ | ❑ | ❑ |
| 6. Approaches problems creatively | ❑ | ❑ | ❑ |
| **C. Efficiency and Productivity** | | | |
| 1. Handles a reasonable volume of work for level of practice and/or complexity of assignment load | ❑ | ❑ | ❑ |
| 2. Performance under pressure | ❑ | ❑ | ❑ |
| 3. Sets priorities | ❑ | ❑ | ❑ |
| 4. Works industriously | ❑ | ❑ | ❑ |
| 5. Sets and meets appropriate deadlines | ❑ | ❑ | ❑ |
| 6. Uses research tools efficiently | ❑ | ❑ | ❑ |
| **D. Communication Skills** | | | |
| 1. Writes clearly, concisely, and persuasively, with correct grammar | ❑ | ❑ | ❑ |
| 2. Written work is neat, properly formatted and carefully proofed | ❑ | ❑ | ❑ |
| 3. Speaks clearly and concisely; receives and holds the attention of others | ❑ | ❑ | ❑ |

| | Exceeds Performance Standards | Meets Performance Standards | Does Not Meet Performance Standards |
|---|---|---|---|
| 4. Communicates at a level appropriate to client personnel and issues involved | ❑ | ❑ | ❑ |
| 5. Communicates proposed solution or constructive approaches, not just problems | ❑ | ❑ | ❑ |

**E. Quality of Work Product and Performance**

| | | | |
|---|---|---|---|
| 1. Prepares for court in timely and efficient manner | ❑ | ❑ | ❑ |
| 2. Maintains professional courtroom demeanor and appearance | ❑ | ❑ | ❑ |
| 3. Litigation skills | ❑ | ❑ | ❑ |
| 4. Negotiates cases to achieve best possible outcome | ❑ | ❑ | ❑ |
| 5. Litigates cases skillfully with necessary and relevant evidence presented in efficient manner | ❑ | ❑ | ❑ |

## II. RISK IDENTIFICATION AND MITIGATION

| | | | |
|---|---|---|---|
| 1. Identifies risk exposure, legal problems and issues beyond case at hand | ❑ | ❑ | ❑ |
| 2. Offers constructive suggestions to clients to mitigate risk exposure | ❑ | ❑ | ❑ |
| 3. Suggests and provides client training as appropriate | ❑ | ❑ | ❑ |

## III. CLIENT RELATIONS

| | | | |
|---|---|---|---|
| 1. Maintains positive client relationships | ❑ | ❑ | ❑ |

| | Exceeds Performance Standards | Meets Performance Standards | Does Not Meet Performance Standards |
|---|---|---|---|
| 2. Responds to clients in timely manner | ❑ | ❑ | ❑ |
| 3. Acquires the confidence and cooperation of the client by demonstration of knowledge, accessibility, practically and timeliness | ❑ | ❑ | ❑ |
| 4. Takes initiative on expanding scope and depth of expertise regarding client | ❑ | ❑ | ❑ |

## IV. TEAMWORK / COLLABORATION

| | | | |
|---|---|---|---|
| 1. Takes full responsibility for all assigned legal matters; seeks assistance and support of other lawyer when appropriate | ❑ | ❑ | ❑ |
| 2. Cooperates with and willingly assists other members of the attorney staff | ❑ | ❑ | ❑ |
| 3. Interacts with support staff professionally and courteously | ❑ | ❑ | ❑ |
| 4. Cooperates and accepts assignments with enthusiasm | ❑ | ❑ | ❑ |

## V. ADMINISTRATIVE SKILLS AND RESPONSIBLITY

| | | | |
|---|---|---|---|
| 1. Punctuality and accountability | ❑ | ❑ | ❑ |
| for keeping office informed of whereabouts during working hours | ❑ | ❑ | ❑ |
| 2. Takes responsibility for prompt completion and delivery of time sheets and absence slips | ❑ | ❑ | ❑ |

| | Exceeds Performance Standards | Meets Performance Standards | Does Not Meet Performance Standards |
|---|---|---|---|
| 3. Compliance with rules, policies and regulations | ❑ | ❑ | ❑ |
| 4. Neatness of work area | ❑ | ❑ | ❑ |

## VI. SUPERVISION RESPONSIBILITIES

**(IF APPLICABLE):**

| | | | |
|---|---|---|---|
| 1. Efficiently plans, assigns and coordinates work | ❑ | ❑ | ❑ |
| 2. Accepts responsibility | ❑ | ❑ | ❑ |
| 3. Trains and leads staff | ❑ | ❑ | ❑ |
| 4. Reinforces Performance Standards with team members | ❑ | ❑ | ❑ |
| 5. Provides adequate and appropriate oversight to team members | ❑ | ❑ | ❑ |
| 6. Is available as a resource | ❑ | ❑ | ❑ |
| 7. Provides clear and adequate instruction | ❑ | ❑ | ❑ |
| 8. Is fair and impartial to staff | ❑ | ❑ | ❑ |
| 9. Is timely in completing supervisory tasks (including performance evaluations) | ❑ | ❑ | ❑ |
| 10. Influences and engenders positive atmosphere | ❑ | ❑ | ❑ |
| 11. Sets good example | ❑ | ❑ | ❑ |
| 12. Encourages the achievement of individual and office goals | ❑ | ❑ | ❑ |

## VII. RATINGS OF GENERAL EMPLOYMENT PERFORMANCE FUNCTIONS

(Check if the following were completed):

| | Exceeds Performance Standards | Meets Performance Standards | Does Not Meet Performance Standards |
|---|---|---|---|
| 1. Maintains consistent attendance | ❑ | ❑ | ❑ |
| 2. Presents professional appearance/ neatness | ❑ | ❑ | ❑ |
| 3. Is cooperative | ❑ | ❑ | ❑ |
| 4. Demonstrates application of effort | ❑ | ❑ | ❑ |
| 5. Shows interest in job | ❑ | ❑ | ❑ |
| 6. Takes initiative | ❑ | ❑ | ❑ |
| 7. Practices positive employee relations | ❑ | ❑ | ❑ |

## SECTION D: GOALS AND OBJECTIVES

❑ Progress and successes on achieving goals and objectives during this rating period are summarized in the attached narrative

❑ Goals and objectives for the next rating period are set forth in a separate memorandum that accompanies this performance evaluation

### EVALUATOR:

I have prepared this evaluation with input from the Chief Deputy and other, and have discussed it with the attorney rated.

________________________________________

(Evaluator's Signature, (DATE)

**ATTORNEY RATED**

**(Please sign either Section A or B Below):**

A. I have discussed this evaluation with the evaluator.

________________________________________

(Attorney's Signature, (Date)

**B. APPEAL**

I have reviewed this evaluation with my supervisor and wish to appeal it in accordance with the performance appraisal provisions of the Civil Service Rules.

________________________________________

(Attorney's Signature, (Date)

**REVIEWED BY:**

________________________________________

(Chief Deputy, (Date)

________________________________________

County Counsel, (Date)

# PERFORMANCE STANDARDS: JUVENILE DEPENDENCY DIVISION

## DEPUTY COUNTY COUNSEL AND SENIOR DEPUTY COUNTY COUNSEL

In order for the juvenile dependency division to meet its goal to deliver the highest quality legal services, attorneys must perform in a professional and competent manner. Performance standards are used to inform attorneys what is expected of them and establish guidelines with which to measure their performance. In addition to the performance standards, the attached performance-based criteria also shall apply to the performance evaluation process. Therefore, all attorneys in the Deputy County Counsel and Senior Deputy County Counsel classifications shall be evaluated in accordance with these performance standards and the performance-based criteria applicable to the attorney being evaluated. A copy of the performance-based criteria is attached.

## I. DELIVERY OF LEGAL SERVICES

### A. Legal Knowledge

Performance standards measure the legal knowledge of the attorney in the delivery of legal services.

### *Function – Attorney Performance Expectations*

***1. Provides thorough, complete and accurate legal advice.***

Gives appropriate and accurate advice to client; is familiar with available research tools; researches legal issues as necessary; checks accuracy of advice as to past advice, new law and other available information.

### *Function – Attorney Performance Expectations*

***2. Demonstrates thorough knowledge of juvenile dependency law***

Studies and develops familiarity with juvenile dependency law; understands legal issues that frequently arise in juvenile dependency cases.

### *Function – Attorney Performance Expectations*

***3. Demonstrates general knowledge of law***

Is knowledgeable of legal issues and areas of law that may be applicable to the practice of juvenile dependency law, including evidentiary law and collateral issues that may arise in trial or appellate work.

### *Function – Attorney Performance Expectations*

***4. Demonstrates initiative in expanding scope and depth of legal knowledge***

Studies materials relevant to juvenile dependency law and other area that may be applicable.

### *Function – Attorney Performance Expectations*

***5. Takes advantage of substantive training opportunities from all available sources***

Participates in training opportunities available, including Joint Law Office Training, in-house training and other training necessary to maintain compliance with statute and rules of court.

### B. ANALYTICAL ABILITIES

Performance standards describe the expected analytical process of the attorney.

*Function – Attorney Performance Expectations*

***1. Identifies relevant facts***

Reviews files of all assigned cases; discusses assigned cases with client; makes use of in-house investigators; obtains necessary documents; identifies necessary witnesses; discusses issues with experts and other attorneys as necessary.

*Function – Attorney Performance Expectations*

***2. Identifies and focuses on critical legal issues, including public policy considerations and County policies***

Evaluates issues raised by clients for relevant legal issues; researches law; applies facts; evaluates policy aspects of issues; evaluates appellate potential.

*Function – Attorney Performance Expectations*

***3. Demonstrates good judgment***

Draws reasonable conclusions from research and analysis; evaluates consequences of decisions and legal advice; demonstrates the ability to narrow issues.

*Function – Attorney Performance Expectations*

***4. Recognizes the gravity and ramification of issues beyond the immediate case***

Evaluates issues for ethical or political factors; advises client and others as appropriate to protect County's interest; inform others including Chief Deputy and client if potential ethical or criminal issues are identified.

*Function – Attorney Performance Expectations*

***5. Analyzes problems thoroughly***

Provides adequate analysis of facts and law; draws clear and concise conclusions.

*Function – Attorney Performance Expectations*

***6. Approaches problems creatively***

Makes use of available expertise, both within and outside the office.

## C. EFFICIENCY AND PRODUCTIVITY

Performance standards match legal skills with workload to assure that the attorney work product meets reasonable client expectations.

*Function – Attorney Performance Expectations*

***1. Handles a reasonable volume of work for level of practice and/or complexity of case load***

Responsible for number of trials/appellate assignments at division and team average.

*Function – Attorney Performance Expectations*

***2. Performs under pressure***

Responds calmly when there are pressing or high priority assignments; helps willingly when workload increases or there are staffing shortages necessitating last minutes coverage.

### *Function – Attorney Performance Expectations*

***3. Set priorities***

Balances assignments with regard to complexity of issues and legal deadlines.

### *Function – Attorney Performance Expectations*

***4. Works industriously***

Uses work time effectively; plans ahead to avoid last minute filing and/or subpoenas.

### *Function – Attorney Performance Expectations*

***5. Sets and meets appropriate deadlines***

Prioritizes assignments; keeps up-to-date and organized calendar.

### *Function – Attorney Performance Expectations*

***6. Uses research tools efficiently***

Make maximum use of available research tools; continues to increase knowledge of available research software.

## D. COMMUNICATION SKILLS

Performance standards evaluate accuracy and effectiveness of the delivery of legal services.

### *Function – Attorney Performance Expectations*

***1. Writes clearly, concisely and persuasively, with correct grammar***

Produces well-written writs, briefs and motions, with appropriate citations and logical and concise flow of facts and arguments leading to a sound legal conclusion.

*Function – Attorney Performance Expectations*

***2. Written work is neat, properly formatted and carefully proofed***

Proofreads written work for content and format prior to finalization.

*Function – Attorney Performance Expectations*

***3. Speaks clearly and concisely; receives and holds attention of other***

Communicates effectively, argues with clarity in court; presents ideas effectively to client.

*Function – Attorney Performance Expectations*

***4. Communicates at a level appropriate to client personnel and issues involved***

Explains issues using understandable terms and language.

*Function – Attorney Performance Expectations*

***5. Communicates proposes solutions or constructive approaches, not just problems***

Discusses issues with clients and other counsel in a manner to help them understand problems and arrive at solutions that narrows and/ or resolves issues.

## E. QUALITY OF WORK PRODUCT AND PERFORMANCE

Performance standards establish benchmarks for acceptable legal work.

*Function – Attorney Performance Expectations*

***1. Prepares for court in timely and efficient manner***

Review files; contacts witnesses and issues subpoenas in sufficient time to identify issues and avoid last minute problems.

## *Function – Attorney Performance Expectations*

***2. Maintains professional courtroom demeanor and appearance***

Dresses professionally, speaks courteously in court, adheres to courtroom procedure and etiquette.

## *Function – Attorney Performance Expectations*

***3. Litigation skills***

Demonstrates ability to draft memoranda; develops trial strategy, recognizes and responds to issues as they arise; demonstrates ability to effectively examine and cross-examine witnesses; presents evidence in concise and logical way; argues position persuasively.

## *Function – Attorney Performance Expectations*

***4. Negotiates cases to achieve best possible outcome***

Meets with counsel representing opposing parties; demonstrates ability to narrow issues and influence case resolutions.

## *Function – Attorney Performance Expectations*

***5. Litigates cases skillfully with necessary and relevant evidence presented in efficient manner***

Makes appropriate objections and responses to objections; demonstrates ability to effectively examine and cross-examine witnesses; presents evidence in concise, logical and persuasive way.

## II. RISK IDENTIFICATION & MITIGATION

Performance standards emphasize the responsibility of the attorney to guide the client away from avoidable litigation.

*Function – Attorney Performance Expectations*

***1. Identifies risk exposure, legal problems and issues beyond case at hand***

Anticipates risk exposure in all phases of litigation; informs office of potential liability issues.

*Function – Attorney Performance Expectations*

***2. Offers constructive suggestions to clients to mitigate risk exposure***

Provides competent legal advice; proposes suggestions to reduce risk ; offers alternatives that reduce the potential of risk.

*Function – Attorney Performance Expectations*

***3. Suggests and provides client training as appropriate***

Informs client of relevant laws, policies and procedures; advises clients regarding compliance with laws; recommends revisions to client practice to secure compliance with law.

## III. CLIENT RELATIONS

Performance standards focus on the needs of the clients.

*Function – Attorney Performance Expectations*

***1. Maintain positive clients relationships***

Communicates with clients when assigned case; clarifies issues; offers constructive suggestions; treats clients with respect and in a professional manner.

### *Function – Attorney Performance Expectations*

***2. Responds to clients in timely manner***

Checks voice mail and e-mail and responds to client questions on a daily basis.

### *Function – Attorney Performance Expectations*

***3. Acquires the confidence and cooperation of clients by demonstration of knowledge, accessibility, practicality and timeliness***

Takes responsibility for legal problems and issues presented by client; advises client of appropriate course of action; advises client of likely results; trains clients when appropriate.

### *Function – Attorney Performance Expectations*

***4. Take initiative on expanding scope and depth of expertise regarding client***

Keeps current in knowledge of client's policies and procedures; keeps current in knowledge and understanding of literature in areas related to social work and juvenile dependency practice.

## IV. TEAMWORK/COLLABORATION

Performance standards promote cooperation and sharing of resources.

### *Function – Attorney Performance Expectations*

***1. Takes full responsibility for all assigned legal matters; seeks assistance and support of other lawyers when appropriate***

Researches and prepares written work and trial strategy with competence; share conclusions and outcomes with peers; consults with attorneys with special expertise as necessary.

### Function – Attorney Performance Expectations

***2. Cooperates with and willingly assists other members of the attorney staff***

Share knowledge and materials with other deputies; offers assistance when there is need.

### Function – Attorney Performance Expectations

***3. Interacts with support staff professionally and courteously***

Works closely with secretaries; is polite and responsive to support staff.

### Function – Attorney Performance Expectations

***4. Cooperates and accepts assignments with enthusiasm***

Accepts responsibility for assignments; handles all assignments willingly.

## V. ADMINISTRATIVE SKILLS & RESPONSIBLITIES

Performance standards describe responsibilities for record keeping and management of the delivery of services.

### Function – Attorney Performance Expectations

***1. Punctuality and accountability for keeping office informed of whereabouts during working hours***

Informs secretary and supervisor of whereabouts during work hours; is on time to assigned court; indicates whereabouts on sign-out board.

*Function – Attorney Performance Expectations*

***2. Takes responsibility for prompt completion and delivery of time sheets and absence slips***

Records work time accurately; obtains approval for absences and overtime in timely manner; submits time sheets in a timely manner.

*Function – Attorney Performance Expectations*

***3. Complies with rules, policies and regulations***

Drafts and achieves challenging and relevant goals; is familiar with division policy practice and procedure and procedures manual; follows county counsel administrative policies

*Function – Attorney Performance Expectations*

***4. Neatness of work area***

Maintains office in orderly condition.

## VI. SUPERVISORY RESPONSIBILITIES (IF APPLICABLE):

Performance standards provide a guide to leadership.

*Function – Attorney Performance Expectations*

***1. Efficiently plans, assigns and coordinates work***

Assigns cases promptly; considers complexity and sensitivity of case; considers experience and skills of assigned deputy; considers availability, time restrictions and requirements; considers workload for individuals and team; reviews and confers with assigned deputy regarding status of cases as appropriate.

## Function – Attorney Performance Expectations

***2. Accepts responsibility***

Accepts and performs supervisorial responsibilities with diligence and enthusiasm.

## Function – Attorney Performance Expectations

***3. Trains and leads staff***

Conducts meetings; sets example through performance; keeps those under supervision advised as to legal developments and procedural issues as they arise.

## Function – Attorney Performance Expectations

***4. Reinforces performance standards with team members***

Provides feedback to deputies; use feedback as basis for evaluations, training, professional development and team building.

## Function – Attorney Performance Expectations

***5. Provides adequate and appropriate oversight to team member and their responsibilities***

Observes deputies under supervision in trial, in oral argument and in calendar; reviews and edits written work of deputies under supervision.

## Function – Attorney Performance Expectations

***6. Is available as a resource***

Share knowledge of law, trial strategy, office policy and procedures; cooperates with other supervisors to help assure coverage of all division assignments and responsibilities.

## *Function – Attorney Performance Expectations*

***7. Provides clear and adequate instruction***

Instructs team members as to expectations; treats team members and support staff fairly and impartially.

## *Function – Attorney Performance Expectations*

***8. Is fair and impartial to staff***

Documents both good and poor quality work; provides feedback to team members regarding written and trial work; communicates criticism constructively and clearly, with written follow-up.

## *Function – Attorney Performance Expectations*

***9. Is timely in completing supervisory tasks (including performance evaluations)***

Attends meeting with Chief Deputy as scheduled; assigns cases promptly; completes evaluations on schedule; sets example by meeting deadlines.

## *Function – Attorney Performance Expectations*

***10. Influences and engenders positive atmosphere***

Gives directions, advice and criticism with courtesy and in constructive manner; supports office policies; encourage team members to be supportive of office policies.

## *Function – Attorney Performance Expectations*

***11. Sets good example***

Drafts and meets relevant and challenging goals; is professional in dress, demeanor and conduct; performs duties and responsibilities accurately, promptly and competently.

*Function – Attorney Performance Expectations*

***12. Encourages the achievement of individuals and office goals***

Discusses goals with those under supervision; keeps apprised of the status of goal achievements of those under supervision; provides feedback from meeting with Chief Deputy to those under supervision.

## VII. GENERAL EMPLOYMENT STANDARDS

Performance standards measure general employment functions.

*Function – Attorney Performance Expectations*

***1. Maintain consistent attendance***

Regularly observes normal working hours; requests time-off (other than unplanned sick leave) in advance.

*Function – Attorney Performance Expectations*

***2. Presents professional appearance/ neatness***

Consistently dressed in a manner, appropriate for a high quality law office; observe casual dress guidelines on Fridays.

*Function – Attorney Performance Expectations*

***3. Is cooperative***

Assists others in performance of job duties; exhibits pleasant demeanor; is courteous in dealing with others; is supportive of fellow workers; contributes to a positive and productive work environment.

## *Function – Attorney Performance Expectations*

### *4. Demonstrates application of effort*

Demonstrates consistent commitment to produce timely and quality work product; takes concerted steps to provide services and work products above and beyond expectations.

## *Function – Attorney Performance Expectations*

### *5. Shows interest in job*

Demonstrates a desire to learn as much as possible in job; volunteers to handle work assignments; participates actively on teams/committees in office; takes advantage of training opportunities; demonstrates commitment and dedication to enhance quality reputation of attorneys in office.

## *Function – Attorney Performance Expectations*

### *6. Take initiative*

Identifies issues and solutions to problems independent of supervisory input; anticipates client's needs; offers assistance to others voluntarily; takes concerted steps to address and resolve potential problems before they occur; suggests ideas/ alternatives to clients independent of request for legal services.

## *Function – Attorney Performance Expectations*

### *7. Practices positive employee relations*

Identifies issues and solutions to problems independent of supervisory input; anticipates client's needs; offers assistance to others voluntarily; suggests idea/alternatives to clients independent of request for legal services.

# ICWA HERITAGE TREE CHART– Columbus, Ohio

Date: ______________________________

Child/ren's Name (DOB):______________________

______________________________

Place of Birth: ______________________________

Note: ______________________________

______________________________

______________________________

Is Applicant Adopted? ❑ Yes ❑ No

Are Parents Adopted? ❑ Yes ❑ No

If answer is yes, list natural parents below.

______________________________

______________________________

**Maternal Great Grandfather:**

______________________________

Tribe & Roll No: ______________________________

Deceased? __________ Year:__________

**Maternal Great Grandmother:**

______________________________

Tribe & Roll No: ______________________________

Deceased? __________ Year:__________

**Maternal Great Grandfather:**

______________________________________________

Tribe & Roll No: ______________________________

Deceased? __________ Year:_________

**Maternal Great Grandmother:**

______________________________________________

Tribe & Roll No: ______________________________

Deceased? __________ Year:_________

**Maternal Grandfather:**

______________________________________________

Tribe & Roll No: ______________________________

DOB: ________________________________________

Deceased? __________ Year:_________

**Maternal Grandmother:**

______________________________________________

Tribe & Roll No: ______________________________

DOB: ________________________________________

Deceased? __________ Year:_________

**Mother:**

______________________________________________

Tribe & Roll No: ______________________________

DOB: ________________________________________

Deceased? __________ Year:_________

**Paternal Great Grandfather:**

______________________________________________

Tribe & Roll No: ______________________________

Deceased? __________ Year:_________

**Paternal Great Grandmother:**

______________________________

Tribe & Roll No: ______________________

Deceased? __________ Year:__________

**Paternal Great Grandfather:**

______________________________

Tribe & Roll No: ______________________

Deceased? __________ Year:__________

**Paternal Great Grandmother:**

______________________________

Tribe & Roll No: ______________________

Deceased? __________ Year:__________

**Paternal Grandfather:**

______________________________

Tribe & Roll No: ______________________

DOB: ______________________________

Deceased? __________ Year:__________

**Paternal Grandmother:**

______________________________

Tribe & Roll No: ______________________

DOB: ______________________________

Deceased? __________ Year:__________

**Father:**

______________________________

Tribe & Roll No: ______________________

DOB: ______________________________

Deceased? __________ Year:__________